Searching for THE Ark OF THE Covenant

Randall Price

EUGENE, OREGON

All Scripture quotations are taken from the New American Standard Bible ®, © 1960, 1962, 1963, 1968, 1971, 1972, 1973, 1975, 1977, 1995 by The Lockman Foundation. Used by permission. (www.Lockman.org)

Cover by Terry Dugan Design, Minneapolis, Minnesota

SEARCHING FOR THE ARK OF THE COVENANT

Published by Harvest House Publishers
Eugene, Oregon 97402

Library of Congress Cataloging-in-Publication Data

Price, Randall.
Searching for the Ark of the Covenant / Randall Price.
p. cm.
Includes bibliographical references and index.
ISBN 0-7369-1052-2 (pbk.)
1. Ark of the Covenant. 2. Temple Mount (Jerusalem) I. Title.
BM657.A8P76 2005
296.4'93—dc22 2004025000

Printed in the United States of America

05 06 07 08 09 10 11 12 13 /VP-KB/ 10 9 8 7 6 5 4 3 2

To Jeri (Shaw) Siddall,

who gave me her daughter
and made me her son.

No man could *search* for more!

Arise, shine; for your light has come,
And the glory of the LORD *has risen upon you.*
ISAIAH 60:1

Her children rise up
and bless her.
PROVERBS 31:28

Acknowledgments

I am in the debt of so many in the production of this book. My friends in Israel continue to offer both kind assistance and necessary criticism in my efforts to interpret Judaism and understand the world of the Bible. Many of these helped initially in the research for my book *In Search of Temple Treasures* (1994), which formed the basis for this new work on the subject of the Ark of the Covenant. Of blessed memory are Chief Rabbi Shlomo Goren and Rabbi Meir Yehuda Getz, who met with me on numerous occasions, often (in the case of Rabbi Getz) at 2:00 A.M., to discuss with me their views on the Ark and share with me their search for it beneath the Temple Mount. I am also indebted to Rabbi Chaim Richman who assisted me in an interview with Rabbi Getz and who has offered me his own insights into the mystery of the Ark over more than a decade. I am also grateful for interviews granted by Drs. Leen Ritmeyer, Dan Bahat, Asher Kaufman, Jim Fleming, and Gershon Salomon; by Mr. Fantahune Melaku and Maru Asmare of the Ethiopian community; by Rabbi Nahman Kahane, Yisrael Ariel, and Mr. Zev Bar-Tov. I also express my appreciation to Dr. Randall Smith of the Tabernacle in the Wilderness exhibit (Israel), Dr. Chuck Missler, the British Museum, the Cairo Museum, Mr. Adnan Husseini and Mr. Sam al-Wad of the Administration of the Waqf and Islamic Affairs, Mr. Randy Yach, Desperado Films, Inc., Mr. Paul Streber, and the Bible Center Theological Vocational School in Breckerfeld, Germany, for photographic assistance or permission to use photographs. Thanks is also due to Miss Amy Stanford, Mr. Zachary Vandermeer, Ken and Theresa Stanford, and Eric Ream for editorial assistance and creation of charts for the book. In this respect, of highest mention are the editorial and production team at Harvest House Publishers, who over the years have become not only professional associates but extended family. Special thanks is made to Mr. Bob Hawkins Jr. (President) and Mrs. Carolyn McCready (Vice President of Editorial) for their continued encouragement to me to write and for their kindness in publishing my writing, to Mr. Steve Miller and Mr. Terry Glaspey for their vision and guidance of my work, Mr. Gene Skinner for his assistance in editing this book, to Miss Betty Fletcher, Mr. Gary Lineburg, and Mrs. Katie Brady for their superb skill in layout and graphics.

Finally, my deepest love goes to my wife, Beverlee, and my family, Elisabeth and Eric Ream, Eleisha and Pavel Tabares, Erin Price, Jonathan Price, and Emilee Price. They have endured with me the pressures of separation and deadlines, which are part of the craft, yet they have always been an encouragement to me through their prayers and hugs. I love you all!

Contents

Introduction

The ring of the phone interrupted what was an otherwise dreary winter day. The caller identified himself as the sheriff of a nearby town and asked for me by name. As unsettled as I was to have an officer of the law in personal pursuit, what happened next was totally alarming. "We have a dead body here," said the sheriff, "and the only name on him is your name!" I can tell you I have never before or since received such a call, and all one can do at such a moment is hang in suspense, waiting for some word of explanation. The officer then told me the dead man's name, which I had never heard before, and said that a notebook he had carried had my name and address in it next to the cryptic abbreviation "A.O.C." If I did not know him, what did I make of these letters and of his having my personal information? Thinking at that moment was difficult, but the strange message "A.O.C." was clearly the key to this mystery. Then it came to me! A.O.C.—Ark of the Covenant! I had recently been interviewed on a national radio program about the search for this ancient artifact in relation to my book *In Search of Temple Treasures*. Apparently this man—by his appearance a vagrant who had died of exposure—had heard the interview and was on his way to find me in order to find out more. Though I am still intrigued by the thought of what kind of meeting we might have had, I remain impressed by his desire to find out more about the mysterious Ark!

The New Testament author of the book of Hebrews reflected a similar zeal when he reverently wrote about the sacred objects of his people's earthly sanctuary and focused his attention on the Ark of the Covenant: "Behind the second veil there was a tabernacle which is called the Holy of Holies, having a golden altar of incense and the ark of the covenant covered on all sides with gold, in which was a golden jar holding the manna, and Aaron's rod which budded, and the tables of the covenant; and above it were the cherubim of glory overshadowing the mercy seat; but of these things we cannot now speak in detail" (Hebrews 9:3-5). I have often wondered why the author felt unable to continue with these details—how I wish he had!—But he obviously desired to do so.

For most people this brief account in the New Testament measures the extent of their knowledge of the holy Ark. But like the author of Hebrews, we are aware that more could be said! The good news is that the Scripture does reveal much more about the Ark and is richly supplemented by history, tradition, and archaeology. The only thing we need to add is the desire to know these details. In this book I have attempted to bring together the literary sources that have recorded these details, to compare the archaeological parallels to the Ark in the religions of the ancient Near East, and to investigate the theories of the Ark's whereabouts, including the claims of explorers and others who have reported finding it in various locations. Throughout this journey we will see how this religious relic of Israel's past continues after 2500 years to be the "holy grail" of the modern age.

For this reason, the Ark of the Covenant, the greatest of all ancient treasures, is also the subject of one of the greatest of all stories. If you, like me, love a good story, you will surely find it here as we unfold the saga of the lost Ark. If you like adventure, you will also enjoy our exploration of the secrets of the ancient past. If you are on a quest for truth, as we all should be, then we will together seek to separate fact from fable in the modern claims concerning the Ark. For my part I have traveled to several continents on the trail of the story of the Ark, interviewing archaeologists, Jewish rabbis, and Ethiopian priests, as well as tracking down the facts behind sensationalist claims. It has been quite a trip, and the journey has not yet ended. But, above all, in searching together for the one object in history that God used to reveal His presence on earth, you and I will have the opportunity to trace its divine outline and understand its holy purpose. To do so is to enter into God's presence and to behold His glory! If you have a desire to know more—and to know Him—follow me in searching for the Ark of the Covenant.

Part 1

Searching for Understanding About the Ark

1
Understanding the Ark

There I will meet with you; and from above
the mercy seat, from between the cherubim
which are upon the ark of the testimony,
I will speak to you about all that I will give you
in commandment for the sons of Israel.

—Exodus 25:22

These words from one of the greatest events in Israel's history also introduce us to the greatest object in Israel's devotion—the Ark of the Covenant. Israel's exodus from Egypt was a transition from national slavery to national sovereignty. The Ark takes its position here at the beginning of Israel's national identity as a symbol of Israel's unique covenant relationship with God. This was demonstrated in two ways. First, the Ark bore the tablets of the covenant—Israel's constitution, which showed the nation's favored status as God's people. Second, the Ark showed that God was willing to share Israel's desert experience and to be their Companion during the journey to the Promised Land. The Lord's presence with the Ark served to constantly remind the Jewish nation that the Lord would not abandon them to suffer slavery among the nations again.

The Lord first revealed this purpose for the Ark on Mount Sinai when He gave Moses its design: "Let them [Israel] construct a sanctuary for Me, that I may dwell among them. According to...the pattern of the tabernacle and the pattern of all its furniture, just so you shall construct it" (Exodus 25:8-9). These verses are followed by the directions for constructing the Ark as the first and preeminent piece of the Tabernacle's furniture. Above the Ark, God would meet with Moses and manifest His glory to His people. So as God formed Israel into a new national entity, calling them to be His people, the Ark went with them as the sign and seal of God's power to perform His promise.

What Is the Ark?

The Ark is approximately three to four feet long and one to two feet high and wide.[1] The Hebrew word used for the Ark, *'aron*, signifies a box or chest.[2] Our English word *Ark,* which comes to us through the Latin *arca* ("chest"), has the same meaning. In Genesis 50:26 the same Hebrew word *('aron)* is used for the coffin (sarcophagus) in which Joseph was buried. This distinction is important because our English Bibles do not distinguish between the ark of Noah and the Ark of the Covenant. The

Author with replica of the Ark in the Holy of Holies of the Tabernacle in the Wilderness located near Kibbutz Almog (Dead Sea, Israel).
Photo courtesy of Randall Smith.

Hebrew uses a different word for Noah's ark, the word *tebah,* which denotes a kind of container used as a vessel.[3] The same word is used of the woven papyrus basket that bore the infant Moses safely on the River Nile.

The biblical text says that the Ark was made of acacia wood (Exodus 25:10). Acacia trees are native to the Sinai Desert, and the wood was considered so durable that the Septuagint (the Greek version of the Old Testament) translated the Hebrew for "acacia wood" as "incorruptible wood." Magnifying this imperishable quality was the pure gold that overlaid the wood (Exodus 25:11). It may have been applied as gilding (like gold leaf); an idea perhaps denoted by the language of Hebrews 9:4 "covered on all sides with gold." This was the method used on wooden furniture of the period as evidenced in finds from Egyptian tombs. Thin leaves of gold were glued to a fine layer of plaster spread over the wood or applied as hammered sheets to the wood with small nails.[4] However, the rabbinical interpretation of the Hebrew term for "overlay" here is more substantial. According to the Talmud, this indicates thin boxes of gold placed on both the inside and outside of the acacia wood,[5] making it a three-layered box.

The multilayered Ark shown with its golden outer box, inner wooden box, and gold lining inside the wooden box.

Inside the Ark

The Ark contained sacred objects that demonstrated God's presence among the Israelites in the desert. They also served as a witness to future generations of God's covenant with His people (see Hebrews 9:4). Pagan shrines held images of their gods, but in the Ark no such image was present. Rather, the objects in the Ark represented God's demonstration of His Word. These objects, according to the biblical text, were the two stone tablets on which were carved the Ten Commandments (Exodus 25:16; see 31:18), the Torah (Pentateuch) written by Moses (Deuteronomy 31:24-26), the almond-wood staff of Aaron the high priest, which had miraculously budded (Numbers 17:10), and a golden pot of the last trace of the heavenly manna that fed the Israelites during their 40-year desert sojourn (Exodus 16:32-35).[6] While all of these were associated at one time with the Ark, only the two tablets remained permanently with the Ark (2 Chronicles 5:10).[7] Rabbinic tradition also affirmed that the Mosaic legislation (the Torah) remained inside (or beside) the Ark. Clearly the presence of these items makes the Ark the most valuable object in Jewish history. The late Rabbi Shlomo Goren, former Ashkenazi Chief Rabbi of Israel, affirmed this when he declared: "The Ark—the *'Aron Ha-brit*—includes the Ten Commandments, [that is,] the broken and unbroken tablets, and the entire scroll written by Moses. It includes every item that is important for the history of the Jews, and it is the highest stage of sanctity we can have."[8]

Testimonies of Judgment and Grace

The historical objects associated with the Ark represented both divine judgment and grace. After Moses broke the tablets, 3000 Israelites died at the hands of the Levites (Exodus 32:28). After the people complained about the manna, a severe plague

A look inside the Ark: restored tablets of the law, Aaron's rod that budded, and the pot of manna. Photo courtesy of Bible Center Theological Vocational School, Breckerfeld, Germany.

destroyed the contentious among them. When Korah and his company rebelled, an earthquake wiped out his family and supporters, and a plague killed an additional 14,700 Israelites. God knew that Israel would continue to sin (Deuteronomy 31:27-29), so the objects associated with these events accompanied the Ark as a legal declaration against Israel's future violations of the covenant (Deuteronomy 31:26). This is particularly true of the Torah scroll, by which Israel was to live (Leviticus 18:5; Nehemiah 9:29; Ezekiel 18:9; 20:11; Luke 10:28; Romans 10:5; Galatians 3:12).

But each of these objects also represented the grace of God. As the psalmist stated after recounting a litany of Israel's sins in the desert, "Nevertheless He looked upon their distress when He heard their cry; and He remembered His covenant for their sake, and relented according to the greatness of His lovingkindness" (Psalm 106:44-45). In token of this lovingkindness (covenant faithfulness), alongside the broken tablets were the second set of restored tablets, indicating God's graciousness to continue His covenant with Israel despite their rebellion with the golden calf (Exodus 34:1-28). The pot of manna also revealed God's loyal love, for God continued His constant care of the nation, giving them all their "daily bread," until they finally reached the Land of promise (Exodus 16:35; Joshua 5:12). Likewise, Aaron's rod that budded was graciously given to validate God's proper priesthood (Numbers 17:5; 18:6-9,23) and therefore preserve the lives of those who would otherwise have perished for their complaints (Numbers 17:10). Finally, the book of the law (the Torah) was present with the Ark to testify to every successive generation (Deuteronomy 4:9) that God had not chosen the nation because of anything in the nation itself but because of His own sovereign love and gracious choice (Deuteronomy 7:6-9).

Each of these objects testified to God's grace and assured Israel of the possibility of divine forgiveness. On the Day of Atonement (Hebrew, Yom Kippur), the high priest sprinkled the blood of the guilt offering upon the mercy seat of the Ark. The Hebrew word for the mercy seat, *kapporet,* is related to this special day because the blood on the lid of the Ark ceremonially "purged" *(Kippur)* the nation of its sin, which was represented by the objects inside. Thus, when God looked down from between the cherubim, He saw only the blood, which turned the Ark from a throne of justice into a throne of grace! The Ark therefore was an ever present testimony of the truth that despite man's sin, God has graciously provided a way of salvation.

The Mercy Seat of the Ark

On top of the Ark was a golden lid known in English as the mercy seat, although the Hebrew term *kapporet* simply signifies a covering. The mercy seat is described as a separate object from the Ark, probably because it required a separate construction. But the command to build the mercy seat immediately follows the command to build the Ark (Exodus 25:17-21), and once they were joined, the mercy seat became inseparable from the Ark and is described this way in every reference to the Ark thereafter. The mercy seat functioned practically as a lid for the box containing the tablets and was held in place by a rim or crown of gold that surrounded the top four corners of the outer box. This assured that if the Ark was jostled in transport, the lid would not fall off and expose the contents of the Ark. In such a case, all those who even inadvertently beheld the Ark might die. Two cherubim formed out of one solid piece of gold topped the golden lid. Medieval Jewish commentator Rashi explained that when the lid was made, a large quantity of gold was poured out and beat in the middle with a hammer or mallet to make the ends bulge upward. The cherubim were then formed from these protruding extremities.

The mercy seat of the Ark showing the rim surrounding the lid and the two cherubim formed at each end. Photo courtesy of Randall Smith.

The Cherubim on the Mercy Seat

Flavius Josephus, the first-century Jewish historian, was from a priestly family and therefore had access to the Second Temple in his day. Although his writings offer an eyewitness description of the inside of the Temple, Josephus remarks concerning the cherubim: "No one can tell what they were like."[9] This statement is curious because the Talmudic tractate *Yoma* 54a records that the walls and tapestries inside the Holy Place of the Temple contained pictorial reproductions of the cherubim. It is strange that Josephus would not know of this detail, especially since he includes so many others, even within the Holy of Holies itself. At any rate, like Josephus, we have no reliable information as to the exact appearance of the cherubim. We can only piece together a possible likeness from biblical, traditional descriptions and archaeological comparisons.

From the biblical use of the Hebrew term *keruvim* (which is only transliterated as "cherubim" in English), we must conclude that these beings are a class of angels like the six-winged seraphim in Isaiah and the four-faced and four-winged cherubim in Ezekiel. However, the cherubim that were positioned on the Ark cover had only one face and two wings each. Their faces were turned inward, and their wings were spread horizontally near their heads. Despite the popular misconception of cherubs as baby angels or cupids (derived from Græco-Roman mythology), they always appear in Scripture as immensely powerful beings that attend the visible presence of God.

The cherubim on the Ark also bore a deep theological significance that reaches back to the Garden of Eden and the fall of man. The earliest mention of the cherubim—and in fact, the only such reference before the construction of the Ark—is in Genesis 3, the story of Adam and Eve's fall. Through the fall, sin had forced the human couple to flee from the holy ground in the garden to the cursed ground outside, which now bore thorns and

Close-up of the cherubim interpreting them with human features and in the posture of worship (covering their faces before God). Photo courtesy of Randall Smith.

thistles, demanded constant toil, and could not keep plants or animals alive forever (Genesis 3:17-19). Adam and Eve were kept from returning to the holy garden in their unholy state by the cherubim stationed at the east entrance to the Garden of Eden. While the sacred tree of life remained, the garden had to be guarded from the defiling intrusion of sin and sinners. Man could not return to God, so he could not return to the garden where God's presence was manifested.

In the fallen world beyond the sanctuary of Eden, God's holy presence was unwelcome. Therefore, the cherubim held flaming swords that turned in every direction, barring any return to God. This representation of fiery judgment warned sinners of their deserved punishment if they attempted to violate that which was holy. At this point, mankind's future appeared bleak. Indeed, even though God chose Abraham to bring blessing to mankind (Genesis 12:3), troubles befell Abraham's children, climaxing with their slavery in Egypt for 400 years. However, at this darkest hour the divine drama goes forward to Sinai. God frees the slaves from bondage and transforms them into a new nation. In this drama of restoration and renewal of covenant, God reveals His plan for mankind—through the inclusion of the cherubim on the Ark.

Without the reference in Genesis to the cherubim, we would have no explanation for their later appearance in the Tabernacle and Temple. At Sinai, the Tabernacle replaced the Garden of Eden. Sinful man still could not return to a holy God, but a holy God had returned to sinful man. At the garden, the cherubim prevented human access to God's presence, but at the Ark, the cherubim welcomed mankind's approach. Even the *position* of the cherubim on the Ark demonstrated this reversal. The cherubim in Eden faced outward, guarding God's presence within the garden from any approach by man. By contrast, the cherubim on the Ark faced inward, turning away from man and toward the place where God's presence was now manifested to man. This is seen in the words of Exodus 25:22: "There I will meet with you; and from above the mercy seat, from between the two cherubim which are upon the ark of the testimony, I will speak to you about all that I will give you in commandment for the sons of Israel." This verse demonstrates the dramatic change in humanity's relationship with God that was accomplished through the Ark.

But the presence of the cherubim also remind us of the unchanging holiness of God. In Exodus 33:20 (see also Deuteronomy 5:25-26) we read that no one could behold God's face (His glory) and remain alive. When God's glory was on top of Mount Sinai, no one, not even an animal, could approach or touch the mountain (Exodus 19:12-24; Hebrews 12:20). If this revelation of God high on a mountaintop could instantly kill, how much more if He took up residence in the very midst of the Israelite camp! Therefore, in order to prevent God's glory from breaking forth upon men, the cherubim were present to guard God's glory, lest in making their approach, men transgressed and defiled the divine presence.

The connection between the Garden of Eden and Sinai was also demonstrated by the direction in which men were to approach God's presence at the Ark. Both the Tabernacle (and later the Temple) were entered from the east, the same position guarded by the cherubim in Eden. Understanding this symbolism, the rabbis declared that "the Ark was in the exact center of the whole world...standing on the starting point of the creation" (Tanhuma, *Kedoshim* 10). Although a return to Eden was impossible, the representative presence of sinful man (through the priesthood) before the holy and all-consuming presence of God's glory was now possible at the Ark.

Touching the Untouchable

Even though man had a new beginning with God at the Ark, man's sinful condition remained and made direct access to God forbidden. Therefore, the Ark, which represented God's presence, was to be treated as holy, and no man was to look upon or touch the Ark once the presence of God had descended upon it. For this reason, the Ark was placed in a dark, windowless room, and when the high priest went before the Lord's presence at the Ark, he had to first fill the room with a heavy cloud of incense to hide the Ark. According to the rabbis, he then had to feel his way to the mercy seat by means of the extended poles of the Ark (always left in place) because he was forbidden to look upon the Ark itself. When the Levites transported the Ark, they had to first cover it with a blue cloth without looking upon or touching it in the process. Only when they had properly covered the Ark could they bring it out in the sight of the Israelites. Many people are disturbed by this "untouchableness" of the Ark. They do not think it fair that God would kill the men of Beth-shemesh who simply gazed in curiosity at the Ark (1 Samuel 6:19) or Uzzah, who tried to prevent it from falling (2 Samuel 6:6-7). Therefore, some people have offered alternative explanations to why people died when they came into contact with the Ark.

Author demonstrating method of high priest's approach to the mercy seat of the Ark by following the poles of the Ark to the place of the offering.
Photo courtesy of Randall Smith.

Explanations of the Ark's Power

One explanation for the deadly effect of the Ark was that it was an ancient battery, charged with high voltage. Anyone who disturbed its energy flow would be instantly electrocuted. Author Richard Andrews described the Ark as a giant capacitor, capable of storing electrical energy. In a 1999 article for the *Daily Mail*, a British newspaper, he stated, "Gold is one of the best conductors of electricity there is, while wood is one of the best insulators.... If the Israelites had set out to construct a primitive accumulator, they could hardly have picked a better design than the Ark."[10] Andrews, who had once been a furniture builder, constructed a replica of the Ark. Tests of his model at a college laboratory confirmed that it could accumulate and release an electrical charge. Andrews theorizes that the friction of the heated air of the desert against the Ark permitted it to accumulate static electricity. "The strength of the charge," he observed, "would depend on variables such as humidity and temperature, but also length, speed and bumpiness of journey...there is no reason why the charge could not be lethal."[11]

A possible example of an ancient battery (though contested) is now in the National Museum of Iraq in Baghdad. Attributed to the Parthian Empire (an ancient Asian culture that ruled most of the Middle East from 247 B.C. to A.D. 228), the object (estimated to be from 200 B.C.) is a clay jar only five inches high and three inches wide. It has an opening sealed with an asphalt plug, which held a copper sheet in place, rolled into a tube. According to Matthew Zymet, who reported on this artifact for The Learning Channel, "This tube was capped at the bottom with a copper disc held in place by more asphalt. A narrow iron rod was stuck through the upper asphalt plug and hung down into the center of the copper tube—not touching any part of it. Fill the jar with an acidic liquid, such as vinegar or fermented grape juice, and you have yourself a battery capable of generating a small current."[12] Experiments with models of the "Baghdad Battery" have demonstrated it can generate between 1.5 and 2 volts. However, these naturalistic explanations for the Ark's power do not explain how someone simply looking at the Ark could be affected (as were the men of Beth-shemesh).

Henry Soltau, a scholar of the last century who wrote books about the Tabernacle and its vessels, believed that those who looked into the Ark were killed because the contents of the Ark were exposed. Inside were the tablets of the law, "the ministration of death," which would have brought "destruction to the thousands of Israel."[13] However, the men of Beth-shemesh's violation of the righteousness codified in the law brought death, not the tablets of the law themselves (see Romans 2:12-16; 3:19-20; 5:13-14,20; 7:7-11).

Therefore, death in connection with the Ark was not a result of the contents or structure of the Ark. People died when they trespassed against God's holiness. One of the categories of serious sin in the Old Testament was violation (Hebrew *ma'al*) of the *sancta* (holy things that were set apart exclusively to God), the sanctuary, or the priests (Leviticus 5:15). The explanation for this commandment is given in Leviticus 10:3: "It is what the LORD spoke, saying, 'By those who come near Me I will be treated as holy, and before all the people I will be honored.'" From our position "short of the glory of God" (Romans 3:23), we may still think it unfair of God to punish with death those who curiously or accidentally made contact with the Ark, but we can at least understand the righteous basis by which He has acted with respect to His own holiness. However, more insight into the motives of the unfortunate men described in these troubling passages about the Ark may help us with our feelings of unfairness.

An Example of Holiness

The men of Beth-shemesh apparently died because their actions were a deliberate attempt to dishonor God. The original text as well as the context imply that they were not simply looking into the Ark in a curious manner but were peering into the Ark with an attitude of arrogance and with a complete disregard for God's commands about the sanctity of the Ark. This is the insight Targum *Jonathan on the Prophets* offers in its explanation of this incident. Actually, two different explanations are given in this interpretive reading of 1 Samuel 6:19—one in the text and the other in the margin. The one in the text says that the men of Beth-shemesh "rejoiced that they had gazed upon the Ark of the Lord *when it was uncovered*." The marginal reading says that the men died "because *they rejoiced at Israel's misfortunes and despised the Ark* of the Lord when it was uncovered." The emphasis of the text is upon the blasphemous act of the men enjoying the sight of the "naked" Ark, since to behold the Ark was akin to beholding God Himself. The emphasis of the marginal reading is upon the treasonous act of coveting their fellow Jews' destruction, an act of derision that mocked the power of the Ark that was pledged to protect them. Both explanations surface an ulterior motive to defame God's glory—a motive that was worthy of divine punishment. Therefore, the Ark did not kill the men of Beth-shemesh or any others who touched it, but rather an offended holy God in heaven whom the Ark represented.

The Approach to God and the Ark

The Ark, as the holiest of these holy things of God, reminds us that the Holy One whom it represents can only be approached in holiness. We cannot come to God as we are any more than the common Israelite could trespass God's sanctity and live. We cannot come with professed religion, for pretenders who wore the priestly robes died just the same. We can only come if we are considered as holy. God made such holiness possible for us through the sacrifice of Christ: "We have been sanctified through the offering of the body of Jesus Christ once for all" (Hebrews 10:10). Jesus, our holy Savior, has made us acceptable to God by covering our sins with His blood and has further qualified us to serve God as priests. Because of the holy work of Christ, those who have faith in Jesus are now considered holy to the Lord: "You are not your own.... For you have been bought with a price: therefore glorify God in your body" (1 Corinthians 6:19-20). Therefore Christians are commanded to not contaminate themselves as God's "holy place" with unholy things (1 Corinthians 5:7-13; 6:9-18; 2 Corinthians 6:14–7:3; 1 Peter 1:14-16).

How Many Arks?

In discussing the description of the Ark, we must consider the Jewish opinion that two Arks existed to house separate sacred items, in particular, the two different sets of stone tablets upon which the Ten Commandments were written. Michael ben Chaim, a publisher of academic books on Egyptian and Near Eastern archaeology and history, argues that God commanded Israel to build two Arks: "The Torah therefore is absolutely clear. There were two arks, two sets of stones [tablets] and in accordance with G-D's orders, the broken stones which G-D gave, were placed in the Golden ark and the stones which Moses cut were placed in the wooden ark."[14] This tradition is based on the statement in Deuteronomy 10:1-3 that Moses was commanded to make "an ark of wood for yourself." Rashi, the medieval Jewish commentator, stated his opinion based on this passage: "This is not the Ark that Bezalel made [the golden Ark], for see now, they did not deal with [the construction of] the Tabernacle until after Yom Kippur [when the Ark was necessary for the atonement ritual], for upon [Moses'] descent from the mountain he commanded [Israel] about the work of [the construction of] the Tabernacle, and Bezalel made the Tabernacle first and only afterwards [did he make] an Ark and [the] furnishings [of the Tabernacle]. It is [thus] found [that] this was a different Ark. This is the one that would go out with them to battle. That one which Bezalel made did not go out to battle, except in the days of Eli, and they were punished because of it, and it was captured."[15] Therefore, according to rabbinic tradition, the golden Ark of Bezalel remained in the Holy of Holies while the wooden ark of Moses was taken out to the battlefield.

One wonders, if this were the case, why the broken tablets were protected within the Ark at the Tabernacle or Temple while the unbroken tablets were taken out in the field where they were subject to capture. Moreover, where was the wooden ark housed? Certainly within the sanctuary, but then why is only one Ark ever mentioned in the biblical text? The lack of a cover on the wooden ark might explain the ease with which the men of Beth-shemesh later looked into the Ark (1 Samuel 6:19), but looking into an already open Ark should not have carried such a severe penalty.

In fact, the text in Deuteronomy 10 does not require that we see Moses' Ark as different from that described in Exodus 25. In Exodus 25:10, God commands that "*they* [the sons of Israel] shall construct an ark of acacia wood," but the previous verse states, "so *you* [Moses] shall construct it." This language does not suggest that the sons of Israel and Moses made two Arks but that each had a part in fulfilling the commandment to make the one and only Ark.

Because the rabbis regarded the first stone tablets as "God's work" and "written by the finger of God" (Exodus 31:18; 32:16), they were more sacred than the second tablets which Moses "cut out for himself" (Deuteronomy 10:1). However, the text here says, "Cut out for yourself two tablets of stone *like the former ones.*" If Moses was to make the second set like the first set, the implication is that he also made the first set. The first tablets "were God's work" (Exodus 32:16), and the second set was also written on by God (Deuteronomy 10:2).

Moreover, the Bible never says what happened to the set of broken stone tablets. Exodus 32:19 simply says that they were shattered at the foot of the mountain. Scripture never implies that the first set was more sacred than the second set or that a separate Ark was required for each. Indeed, all of the references to the Ark in the Bible are singular and show a continuity for the Ark from Moses' time onward. The New Testament likewise recognizes the one Ark (Hebrews 9:4-5). Likewise, Talmudic tradition stated that both the whole and the broken tablets were contained in one single Ark (*Berakot* 8b; *Baba Bathra* 14b).[16] However, we need not suppose that any pieces of the first set of tablets were preserved and included alongside the restored tablets within the Ark or that two Arks were made to house two sets of stones.

The Aim of the Ark

The aim of the Ark, simply put, was to manifest God on earth. This is seen by the various terms used of the Ark, such as "the ark of the LORD, the Lord of all the earth" (Joshua 3:13), "the ark of the God of Israel" (1 Samuel 5:7), "the ark of the Lord GOD" (1 Kings 2:26), and "the holy ark" (2 Chronicles 35:3). God could only dwell with man on the basis of a covenant, and this is also reflected by other names the Ark bore: "the ark of the testimony" (Exodus 25:22) and "the ark of the covenant of the LORD" (Numbers 10:33; Judges 20:27). The law forbids the making of images of God, so the next best thing would be something that presented God's nature without form. The glory cloud (called in later Jewish literature the Shekinah)[17] confirmed God's presence for a time, but the tablets of the law within the Ark revealed God through His word for all time. Conservative scholars on the subject of the Ark have made the point well:

> What would have been better adapted to make the presence of God felt as a reality than the stone tablets with the Ten Words, through which the Lord had made known to His people His ethical character? For the words on these tablets were a kind of spiritual portrait of the God of Israel, who could not be pictured in bodily form, but whose living, holy presence was a vital element in His people's daily life.[18]

Perhaps for this reason they were said to have been "written by the finger of God" (Exodus 31:18; 32:15-16; 34:1,28; Deuteronomy 9:10). Therefore, more than any other communication from God to men, the tablets were direct evidence of God and of His relationship to Israel.

Thus far, we have seen that the Ark represented God's powerful presence among His chosen people. Enthroned above the guardian cherubim, His feet symbolically rested on the Ark, His footstool. In this way the God of Israel maintained His faithfulness to His covenant with the nation, deposited within the Ark. The objects that attended the Ark rehearsed both the tragedy of judgment and triumph of grace. The tablets of the law and the Torah scroll remained a perpetual witness against the nation's tendency to depart from the provisions of the covenant. The mercy seat provided a way for a holy God to live in the midst of an unholy people. By the atonement made there, God cleansed the national sins of Israel and sanctified them for renewed service as a priestly nation. With this understanding of the purpose of the Ark, let us examine its extraordinary activity within Israel.

The Activities of the Ark

The Ark performed a number of different functions at the same time.[19] These activities related first to God's people and then to other peoples in their association with Israel. In 1 Samuel 6:10–7:2 this association is negative: Those at war with Israel capture the Ark and experience its destructive power. Nevertheless, in 1 Kings 8:41-43 this association is positive, as those outside Israel pray toward the Temple, which houses the Ark. This is important to observe, for if the Ark has a prophetic destiny, it will have it first with respect to the Jewish people but also to Gentiles as well. What are some of these functions of the Ark that have made it the mystery of the ages?

A Passageway of Power

First and foremost, the Ark served as a conduit to channel the power of God among His people. It was an extension of God wherever it went. We see this demonstrated when the Ark was brought into the Jordan River and the waters immediately parted while the Israelites crossed (Joshua 3:8–4:11). In this way, God showed that He was with this new generation of Jews as He had been with their fathers at the crossing of the Red Sea. We see this again at Jericho when the Ark led the way in the supernatural destruction of that city (Joshua 6:6-21). Likewise, whenever the Ark was brought onto the field of battle, both Israel and its enemies attributed the outcome to the Ark (Numbers 14:44; 1 Samuel 4:8,17-22; 5:2-12; 2 Samuel 11:11).

God's power as mediated through the Ark could be either for cursing or for blessing. People who treated the Ark without regard to God's specific commandments concerning its use were cursed. Therefore, when the men of Beth-shemesh lined up to peer into the uncovered Ark (1 Samuel 6:19), or when Uzzah reached out to steady the improperly transported Ark (2 Samuel 6:6-7), the result was instant death. On the other hand, when those such as Abinadab (1 Samuel 7:1-2) or Obed-edom (2 Samuel 6:11-12) properly cared for the Ark at their homes, God blessed them.

A Focal Point of Prayer

The divine presence dwelt tangibly with Israel through the Ark. It represented the point of contact between heaven and earth where God would meet with man. With this understanding, the medieval Jewish legal expert Rambam, in the introduction to his *Terumah,* stated that the Ark was "the focus of all their [Israel's] prayers." In support of this Rambam cites 2 Chronicles 6:32-33 (see 1 Kings 8:42-43). In King Solomon's prayer of dedication at the installation of the Ark into the First Temple, he asked that when people prayed toward the Temple, that God would hear from heaven, His dwelling place, and act upon the requests. Rambam apparently recognized the Ark as a place where heaven met earth, where prayer gained an audience with the Almighty in His heavenly Temple. For this reason, many of the rabbis believed that the celestial Temple was spatially situated directly above the Jerusalem Temple. Therefore, at this one site on earth, the two spheres of the temporal and the eternal were joined at the Ark. If prayers coming from any place on earth were directed toward Jerusalem, they were guaranteed an audience (see 1 Kings 8:47; 2 Chronicles 6:38; Daniel 6:10).

A Gateway to God

Just as the Ark channeled God's power and assured answered prayer, so it also revealed His will. As a veritable "gateway to God," the Ark was a means by which God guided His people. In Exodus 25:22, God told Moses that He would meet with him at the Ark and speak to him there. English translations of the Hebrew term used for the tent where Moses went for these divine encounters have varied. Christian versions usually emphasize the aspect of appointment in their rendering of this word as "tent of *meeting*." Jewish versions, on the other hand, have focused on the aspect of the speaking and so translate the word as "communion tent." Numbers 7:89 depicts Moses coming to the Ark to receive instruction for Israel and hearing the voice of God speaking from between the cherubim. For this reason, some have called the Ark a "divination or oracle box."[20]

Some scholars have suggested that later God revealed the future to high priests who approached the Ark with their ephod, breastplate, and the Urim and Thummim.[21] Perhaps the reason that the heads of tribes and the Levites assembled before Joshua and Eleazar the high priest at Shiloh for a divine decision was that the Ark was stationed there (Joshua 21:1-2). In the days of the Judges, the Ark was apparently used for this purpose, for Judges 20:27 notes, "The sons of Israel inquired of the LORD (for the ark of the covenant of God was there in those days)." In addition, when the boy Samuel was sleeping near the Ark, God summoned and spoke to him (1 Samuel 3:3-21).

We should probably not consider this function of the Ark to be a primary function because Exodus 25:22 does not indicate that meeting to hear God speaking would be a regular activity.[22] More likely, this might have been simply a promise that God would speak to Moses after the dedication of the Tabernacle as a one-time event, as a climax to the ceremonies. If this was so, then Numbers 7:89 would be the fulfillment of that promise and not an example of a typical meeting. However, even if this were a singular event, the tent of meeting and the Ark served as a rallying point for the people, where they met to receive divine revelation as mediated by Moses or by the high priest (1 Samuel 3:1,21). In this way, then, the Ark functioned as a conduit of communication.

God in a Box?

So when we get to the bottom of this box we call the Ark, we have really discovered the greatest treasure of all—God. Imagine, God in a box! In saying this, let us be careful to point out that God was never contained in the Ark. King Solomon made this clear in 1 Kings 8:27, when he acknowledged, "But will God indeed dwell on the earth? Behold, heaven and the highest heaven cannot contain You, how much less this house which I have built!" Solomon was quite aware that when his prayers were directed to the Ark, God would hear in His dwelling place in heaven (1 Kings 8:30). Therefore, while God in His omnipresence filled both heaven and earth (see Isaiah 66:1) and remained in His heavenly Temple (see Psalm 11:4; 20:6), the Ark was the means by which God *manifested* His presence on earth. Whether or not the Jewish people were conscious of this theological distinction, all were quite aware that God's presence attended the Ark!

The presence of God with the Ark and the Ark's concealment created an aura of mystery around this sacred object. This mystery was magnified by the terrible stories of the awesome power that appeared to accompany the Ark into battle and of the quick deaths of those who violated the commandment against touching it. As a result, after the Ark had disappeared, its history became embellished by myth and legend. While the legends have made stories of the Ark more entertaining for fantasy writers and movie producers, we should see the Ark as it really is. Therefore, come with me into the next chapter as we separate fable from fact in our search for the Ark.

2
Fables and Facts About the Ark

Facts become history,
history becomes legend,
and legend becomes myth.

—J.R.R. TOLKIEN, *THE FELLOWSHIP OF THE RING*

The massive accumulation of myths about the Ark in literature, including modern fictional novels and Hollywood scripts, testifies that what began as fact can eventually become fable. The Ark, perhaps more than any other mystery of the ancient past, attracts the storyteller because of its unearthly connection with the divine. It is the one and only object at which God revealed His glorious presence and through which He unleashed His awesome power. Moreover, its central position within the Holy of Holies in the Temple, itself a wonder of the ancient world, gave it an air of being older than time itself, as Jewish tradition affirmed: "The Ark was in the exact center of the whole world...standing on the starting point of the creation" (Tanhuma, *Kedoshim* 10). The Ark's pivotal place helps us understand why the Ark was seen throughout history as the stuff legends are made of.

As we continue our search to understand the Ark, we must separate the facts of the biblical description of the Ark from the fiction of later stories that have come to us. I have isolated three myths about the Ark. First, we will consider the source of the Ark's destructive power. Then we will look at the Ark's alleged ability to transport people from one place to another. Finally we will examine the claim that the Ark was translated to heaven.

Fable: The Ark Was a Superweapon

Scripture depicts the Ark as helping Israel in its conquest of Canaan by parting the Jordan River (Joshua 3:8-17) and causing the walls of Jericho to fall (Joshua 6:2-20). Israel resorted to it for victory in other conflicts (Joshua 10:9-15; 22:13) and in the civil war between Israel and Benjamin (Judges 20:18,26-28). These biblical accounts of the Ark taken into battle to rout the armies of Israel's enemies spawned extrabiblical embellishments of its destructive powers. These supernatural powers supposedly repelled foreign forces and demonstrated the presence of God. One tradition describes the Ark as a mighty and undefeatable weapon of warfare. Two fiery jets allegedly issued from between the cherubim above the Ark, burning up snakes, scorpions, thorns, and enemies in the Israelites' path. Such legendary attributes of the Ark may indicate that people thought it had an independent power apart from God. This kind of thinking exists today, largely due to the influence of sensationalists and the Hollywood film industry. Examples of the first category include books by Erich Von Däniken and television documentaries based on them first aired some two decades ago. Von Däniken believed God was an ancient astronaut and that the earth had originally been colonized by extraterrestrials. He tried to prove that the Bible, as well as other ancient records, cryptically referred to these aliens and their advanced technology. In his first book, *Chariots of the Gods,* he explained that he believed the Ark of the Covenant was an alien invention that was electrically charged.

> If we reconstruct it today according to the instructions handed down by Moses, an electric conductor of several hundred volts is produced. The border and golden crown would have served to charge the condenser that was formed by the gold plates and a positive and negative conductor. If, in addition, one of the two cherubim on the mercy seat acted as a magnet, the loudspeaker—perhaps even a kind of set for communication between Moses and the spaceship—was perfect.[1]

Even Hasidic Jewish scholars have advocated something like this, although on a spiritual level. Akiva Bernstein writes this:

> There are four forces in the universe: the gravitational force, the electromagnetic force, the strong nuclear force, and the weak nuclear force.... We can easily find a correspondence between four of the service vessels and the four forces, as follows: the Shulchan corresponds to the gravitational force, the Menorah corresponds to the electromagnetic force, the Golden Altar corresponds to the strong nuclear force, and the Copper Altar to the weak nuclear force. What, you may ask, does the Ark correspond to? The answer is what is called, in physics, the "Unified Field," the "master field" which is a combination of the other four force types.[2]

This kind of imaginative theory requires no refutation because it offers no evidence to refute. Exact models of the Ark that have been made (on a reduced scale) to the biblical specifications have not produced a significant electrical charge. Furthermore, a great many Egyptian relics (in mint condition) duplicate the Ark's design and serve to prove only that this style (and technology) was typical to the period, not extraterrestrial or wielding unearthly powers.

Nevertheless, Hollywood has perpetuated this concept, principally through producer Steven Spielberg in his film *Raiders of the Lost Ark*. In the opening sequences of the movie, Indiana Jones shows U.S. intelligence officials an old Bible with a flyleaf that has an illustration of the Ark going into battle while emitting rays that destroy the enemy. In the film, a museum curator, Indy's usual sponsor and patron, observes that "the Bible says that the Ark could level mountains and destroy whole regions." Following this premise, the whole plot of the movie is built upon the idea that the Nazis want to find this superweapon and use it against the Allies. In the final sequence, combining the electromagnetic theory with the end-time plague punishment of Zechariah 14:12, Spielberg portrayed the empty Ark as an occultic device that channeled demonic spirits and consumed those who looked at the Ark with fiery destruction.

Fact: The Lord Was a Superweapon

The Bible condemns this very kind of superstitious thinking about the Ark. Rather than having an innate power as a superweapon, the Ark was powerless to prevent its own capture by the enemy. After the Israelites recoil from losing 4000 men in battle, their elders draw the presumptuous conclusion that "the LORD defeated us today before the Philistines." Seeking somehow to circumvent the Lord in the next engagement, they decide to "take to ourselves from Shiloh the ark of the covenant of the LORD, that it may come among us and deliver us from the power of our enemies" (1 Samuel 4:3).

Did these Israelites really believe that the Ark of the Lord could do for them what the Lord of the Ark would not? Maybe they thought that God would be forced to deliver them if His Ark was on the field. The biblical account implies that only the Philistines had a correct understanding of the Ark! When it was brought into the camp they said, "God has come into the camp," and "Woe to us! Who shall deliver us from the hand of these mighty gods? These are the gods who smote the Egyptians" (verses 7-8). Whatever the Israelites' twisted reasoning, the result was that God showed them how their faith was misplaced, not only by letting 30,000 more Israelites die, including the high priest and his successors, but also by allowing the Ark to be taken by the enemy (verses 10-18).

We need not look for a mechanism within the structure of the Ark itself for its slaying power. God directly killed others for acts of disobedience or desecration (see Genesis 38:9-10; Leviticus 10:1-3; Numbers 16:19-33; Acts 5:1-10). God was always and only the true source of the power of the Ark. When the Ark went out to battle, God's presence was thought to go from it to dispel the enemy and then return (Numbers 10:35-36; see Psalm 68:2). When He was not present with it, it was as powerless as any other man-made object. The Bible reminds us that "without faith it is impossible to please Him" (Hebrews 11:6), and God showed His displeasure at Israel's superstition by withdrawing His presence from the Ark. Today, as then, the real tragedy is that people who profess faith still go out to do battle with God's enemies without realizing that He is gone! They charge forth in their own strength, sometimes with superweapons of their own invention, but they return defeated. If God were to remove His Spirit from the world, would church programs and missionary endeavors continue right on, never knowing anything had changed? Let us learn from the Ark to separate fiction from faith and find our deliverance in the Lord.

Fable: The Ark Was a Flying Machine

Jewish legend has also pictured the Ark as a flying device that hovered vertically and moved horizontally through the air. The biblical account of the Ark going before the Israelites in their march through the wilderness has been embellished to explain how this action convinced the Jews of God's presence. The Shekinah was likely not visible to all of the camp, so it was thought that the Ark, which symbolized God's presence, in fact *contained* the divine presence and could be accessed for supernatural assistance. A rabbinical treatment of the prayer of Moses in Numbers 10:35-36 interprets Moses' petition to the Lord as a call to the Ark to demonstrate its powers:

> Do what the Shekinah bids you do [i.e. break camp and move]. But they would not believe Moses that the Shekinah dwelt among them unless he spoke the words: "Rise up, Lord, and let Thine enemies be scattered; and let them that hate Thee flee before Thee," whereupon the Ark would begin to move, and they were convinced of the presence of the Shekinah.[3]

This movement was then described in detail. The Ark was said to have given the signal for breaking camp by soaring up high, and then rapidly moving before the Israelites for a distance of three miles until it found the next proper place for the camp.[4]

The fourteenth-century A.D. Ethiopian Royal Chronicles or national epic known as the *Kebra Negast* ("Glory of the Kings") tells a similar tale of a different company in the presence of the Ark. In this account, which Ethiopians regard as factual history, the supposed son of the Queen of Sheba and King Solomon, Menelik I, is transported through the air from Jerusalem to Ethiopia by the Ark, along with his full entourage of men, horses, camels, and supplies. Filled with stories of other similarly incredible acts by the Ark (see chapter 7), the *Kebra Negast* has been called by historians "legendary propaganda." Its purpose was to validate the claims of royal dynastic succession by a line of Abyssinian Christian rulers in Ethiopia. The Jewish legends were already ancient by the time the *Kebra Negast* was penned, and they probably inspired the Ethiopian version.

Fact: The Beings Associated with the Ark Flew

Flying, or being mystically transported from place to place, is a common theme in many legends of the Near East (especially Muslim). The idea was to symbolize the supernatural element in the story, although the storytellers probably did intend to be interpreted literally. The Bible records similar accounts of supernatural transportations that were accomplished by the Spirit of God (see Ezekiel 3:12-14; 11:1; Acts 8:39), however, these are usually visionary (as Ezekiel 8:3 states) or a means of divine guidance, and not literal transport. One exception is Elijah's translation (2 Kings 2:11), but this was performed by the heavenly (angelic) chariot and had no association with the Ark. The Ark was perhaps symbolic of God's heavenly chariot by which He moved from place to place (Psalm 68:17; Isaiah 66:15; Ezekiel 1; 10:6-22; see 2 Chronicles 28:18), but Scripture never refers to the Ark as a symbolic (and certainly not a literal) means of aerial conveyance. The angel of the presence, not the Ark, accompanied the glory cloud that lifted up and moved before the Israelites (Exodus 14:19; 23:20-23; 32:34). And this same Shekinah, accompanied by heavenly cherubim, departed in flight over the Mount of Olives (Ezekiel 11:23). Therefore, the biblical evidence shows that legitimate cases of the power of flight are connected with angelic beings and have no direct connection with the Ark itself.

Fable: The Ark Was Transported to Heaven

The failure to find the Ark on earth has led some to conjecture that it might have been taken to heaven. This belief is shared by some Jews as well as Christians, although on different grounds. According to J.M.P. Otts, "The Jews have a tradition that the Ark was miraculously translated to heaven when Nebuchadnezzar captured the temple, and that it will be restored to earth by the Messiah when he comes."[5] This view is held today by Hasidic Judaism and is part of its belief that nothing related to the ancient Temple, including the Temple itself, was destroyed, but will be restored in the end time (see chapter 11). A similar Christian view exists:

> [The Ark of the Covenant] was safely stored in the heavenly temple. No doubt the Ten commandments are there as well. If God could translate Enoch and Elijah to heaven, and if the resurrected Christ could ascend to heaven, He would be quite able to have an angel remove the ark from Jerusalem before Nebuchadnezzar's armies sacked the temple, and then have him carry it safely to the true tabernacle in the New Jerusalem under construction in heaven.[6]

Because the view claims biblical support, we will examine the scriptural texts used for this argument.

In Revelation 11:19, John declares that he saw the Ark revealed in the heavenly realm: "And the temple of God which is in heaven was opened; and the ark of His covenant appeared in His Temple." Many excellent commentators, eager to reconcile the disappearance of the Ark in the past with this appearance in the future, have quickly made an identification with the lost Ark. This quote is characteristic of such reasoning:

> Just as Yahweh is said to have personally buried Moses with His own hand (Deuteronomy 34:5-6)—lest the body of Moses become an object of national veneration, as is the case with the body of Lenin in Moscow—so the testimony of the Apocalypse is that God returned the Ark of the Covenant to Himself. There it remains to be revealed at the final theophany on the last day (Apocalypse 11:19).[7]

On the surface, this view offers an attractive solution to the problem of the Ark. It seeks to perpetuate the existence and sanctified purpose of the Ark without historical interruption—in the heavenly realm. On closer examination, however, the preservation of the earthly Ark in heaven forces the question of other Temple vessels that also appear in heaven, including the golden altar, incense, censers, harps, bowls, trumpets, and ephods (Revelation 5:8; 7:9,14-15; 8:2-5; 15:2,5-7). And this is not to mention the heavenly appearance of the Tabernacle, tent, and Temple!

If we assume that the Ark was translated into heaven, should we not assume that all of these—equally a part of the Temple worship system—were also translated to heaven? After all, no physical trace of the actual earthly Temple has ever been discovered. Perhaps the report of its destruction by the Romans, being extrabiblical, was a legend, and instead it was carried to heaven to become the Temple that John saw. As mentioned above, some Hasidic rabbis did hold that the entire Temple had been supernaturally removed to heaven and will be preserved until the last days, but this was because they could not conceive of the holy place as actually having been destroyed.

How then do we account for the clear statements of John that the Ark and the Temple appeared in heaven? The answer to this is that the Ark that John saw is the heavenly Ark, which has always existed in the heavenly Temple with God. This heavenly Temple, complete with its vessels, appears at crucial intervals in Revelation.[8] This heavenly Temple is not the same as the earthly Temple (see Psalm 11:4). Scripture is quite clear about this distinction, explaining that the earthly Ark and the Tabernacle and Temple are copies of the originals in heaven (Exodus 25:8-9,40; 1 Chronicles 28:11-19; Hebrews 9:23-24). John also makes this clear in this very context when he speaks of measuring the Temple in Jerusalem but not its outer court, which is reserved "to be trodden down by the nations" (Revelation 11:1-2). Because this Temple exists at the same time as the Temple in heaven, they cannot be the same structure.

Fables are plentiful, but because they sprout from the original stock of fact, the two can only be successfully separated if attention is given to the root. But as the Greek philosopher Thucydides once said, "Most people do not take pains to get to the truth of things, but believe the first thing they hear." However, though new fables will surely sprout concerning the Ark, you have taken pains to come this far, so surely you will get to the truth of the things you will hear! As our search for the Ark continues, we must now search in the realm of archaeology to see if the ancient world into which the Ark came can help us in better understanding its appearance and action.

3

What Does Archaeology Reveal About the Ark?

The real business of archaeology is to establish benchmarks in the world of the Bible to guide interpreters.

—JOSEPH CALLAWAY

The fables connected with the Ark have often left the impression that the Ark lacks historicity. Skeptics who reject the historicity of the Bible itself of course reject the historicity of the Ark since it is part of the miraculous events recorded there. For example, Jordan Maxwell of the University of Southern California brands the Ark as pure fiction: "There never was an Ark of the Covenant. It's as fictional as the search for it by Indiana Jones in *Raiders of the Lost Ark*. As serious scholars, we can all stop looking for that lost Ark of the Covenant and leave it to Hollywood, because that's where it belongs, in the realm of fantasy!"[1] Indeed, the miraculous events associated with the Ark—parting rivers, bringing down impregnable walls, destroying enemy cities, and instantly liquidating idolaters and the irreverent—destined it to become a subject for Hollywood scriptwriters. On this same basis, critical scholars have argued that the Ark is simply a literary creation, a piece of religious fiction designed for a theological drama. But if such an association relegates the Ark to the sphere of sacred superstition, its association with actual archaeological artifacts transfers it from the realm of fiction to that of fact.

Archaeological Parallels to the Ark

Archaeological studies in the Near East offer numerous parallels to the Ark that demonstrate its reality. From archaeology, we are able to confirm its appearance and purpose in relation to the biblical text, a comparison that argues in turn for the historicity of the Bible itself. Ancient Egyptian processional barques (scale models of Nile boats that carried statues of the gods) offer examples of objects similar in form and function to the Ark. We have seen that the Hebrew word for "ark" *('aron)* was used of Egyptian coffins (Genesis 50:26), and some Egyptian sarcophagi, such as that of Osiris (adorned with a pair of winged figures), and articles entombed with the mummies have arklike appearances. For example, the Cairo Museum displays objects from the tomb of the young Egyptian pharaoh Tutankhamen

Portable wooden ark (with carrying poles) from the tomb of Tutankhamen. Photo by author. Courtesy of Cairo Museum.

(1400 B.C.). Several of Tutankhamen's treasures have much in common with the biblical description of the wooden chest that formed the larger part of the Ark.[2] One of these portable Egyptian "arks" is a chest of cedar 32 inches long with wooden transport poles that slid through brass rings attached underneath. Another is a large gilded shrine with carrying poles topped with an image of the god Anubis. Other ancient Near Eastern cultures also provide similar examples, such as the Tammuz chest of the Babylonians, the step shrines of the Hittites and Nabateans (such as that at Petra), and Canaanite ceramic miniature temples at Megiddo.

Gilded arklike shrine of Anubis. Photo by author. Courtesy of Cairo Museum.

Parallels to the mercy seat and cherubim figures above the Ark also appear in many Near Eastern cultures. Egyptian sphinxes, usually appearing in pairs, adorn many ritual objects, including "arks," although in most cases they are engraved on the sides of these chests. Monumental statues of sphinxes, winged bulls, and griffins come from Assyria and Syria, Babylon, Persia, Greece, and Phoenicia, and smaller depictions have also come from Canaan and Israel. The monumental figures are usually found guarding the entrances to palaces or temples. The Syrian and Israelite examples represent exquisitely detailed ivories such as those discovered in the palace of the Assyrian governor of Hadatu at Aslan Tash in northern Syria[3] and those from the Israelite King Ahab's palace in Samaria. The figures on these objects appear as a combination of animal and human: a lion and a man (in Egypt), a winged bull and a man (in Babylon), and a winged lion and a man (in Syria and Israel). In the religions of these countries, human and animal attributes were combined to represent the powerful guardians of the gods. To what degree any of these represent the cherubim of the Ark is difficult to decide. Those from Samaria might have been expected to reproduce those of the Temple in Jerusalem, but given the apostasy under King Ahab, the Samarian images were more likely influenced by local pagan mythology. Those on the Ark, which were copies of the heavenly reality (Exodus 25:9,40), were distinctive in their representation, as the Talmud implies:

> Rav Katina said: "When the Jewish people would go up to Jerusalem during the Festivals, the Keepers of the Sanctuary would roll back the curtain covering the Holy Ark, and would reveal to the Jews who came up to Jerusalem, the cherubs, which were in the form of a male and female, embracing each other. And they would say to them, to the Jews: 'See the love which G-d has for you, like the love of a male and female' " (*Yoma* 54a).

Another Jewish tradition says that the cherubs had the face of small children, the symbol of Jewish continuity. While these statements may be more pedagogical than historical, they show that the cherubim were unique in the ancient Near East.

Archaeology and the Concept of the Ark

The Bible portrays the Ark as the place where the God of heaven touches earth. For example, we read of "the ark of the covenant of the LORD of hosts *who sits above the cherubim*" (see 1 Samuel 4:4; 2 Samuel 6:2; 2 Kings 19:15; Psalm 80:2; 99:1; Isaiah 37:16). Therefore, Scripture often refers to it as "the *footstool* of our God" (see 1 Chronicles 28:2; Psalm 132:7-8). This concept is illustrated in the ancient art of Israel's closest neighbors in Syria and Canaan.[4] In Assyrian and Babylonian reliefs, a king is usually attended by a representation of a deity that appears as a winged solar disk hovering above his head (see for example the relief of King Darius on Mount Behistun). At Byblus, Hamath, and Megiddo, researchers have found representations of a king seated on a throne flanked by winged creatures. A tenth-century B.C. example depicts King Hiram of Byblus seated on his cherubic throne.[5] Similar images of the Megiddo ivories are of particular interest because they reflect Phoenician craftsmanship, such as was employed in building both the First and Second Temples (1 Kings 5; Ezra 3:7). These may give the nearest representation to those on the Ark. The purpose for this symbolism was to show the divine status of the one on the throne, riding upon a heavenly chariot attended by a retinue of celestial beings (2 Samuel 22:11; Psalm 18:10). We see further parallels in the function of the Ark as the repository of a law code.

Archaeology and the Contents of the Ark

The Ark contained sacred objects associated with God's presence with Israel in the desert. These served as a witness to future generations of the Mosaic covenant. In Near Eastern religions, sacred shrines held images of the gods. But in Israel, physical representations of God were forbidden, so His divine image was communicated through His law contained within the Ark. This law was comprised of ten words (the Ten Commandments) inscribed on a pair of stone tablets. These "tablets of the law" remained a permanent fixture within the Ark (2 Chronicles 5:10).[6] The Hollywood depiction of these tablets is usually monumental. Whether intentionally or not, the cinemagraphic portrayal of an 80-year-old man hefting huge stone slabs weighing hundreds of pounds down a rugged mountain makes the Bible seem more fantasy than reality.

Archaeology, however, offers a more accurate picture. Based on discoveries of similarly inscribed stone tablets, the Ten Commandments were probably carved on stone flakes not much larger than the size of a man's hand.[7] This size is implied by the relatively small size of the Ark itself. In a debate between the two rabbinic sages Rabbi Meir and Rabbi Yehudah, the former said that the stone tablets and the Torah scrolls were placed side by side within the Ark. The latter contended that in the fortieth year of the desert sojourn, a shelf was attached to an exterior side of the Ark to hold the Torah scroll.[8] Either way, only tablets like those just described could have fit within the Ark.

Archaeology also helps us to understand the reason why these tablets were deposited within the Ark. In Near Eastern cultures of Moses' time, the custom was to put legal documents and agreements between rival kingdoms at the feet of their god in their sanctuary. This god acted as the guardian of treaties and

Author displays stone flakes (from the Judean desert) resembling the tablets that contained the Ten Commandments within the Ark.

supervised their implementation. Egyptian records provide an example of this in a pact between Rameses II and Hattusilis III. Their concord was sealed by depositing a treaty both at the feet of the Hittite king's god Teshup and the pharaoh's god Ra. The tablets of the law set within the Ark were likewise at the feet of God in the sense that the Ark was His footstool.

The prophet Samuel followed this tradition by recording the ordinances of the kingdom and setting them "before the LORD," that is, at the foot of the Ark (1 Samuel 10:25). King Hezekiah too may have been acting in accordance with this custom when he "spread out before the LORD" the threatening letter of Rabshakeh the Assyrian (Isaiah 37:14).

Did Pagan Design Influence Israelite Construction?

The Ark was made by Hebrew craftsmen who had lived and worked their entire lives in Egypt, so many people have assumed that the Ark's construction was influenced by Egyptian design. Whether or not this was the case, this would not have applied to the cherubim, since Egyptian sphinxes, like comparable figures in other Near Eastern civilizations, were religious symbols. The first-century Jewish author Flavius Josephus, aware of these other pagan designs, nevertheless stated concerning the cherubim: "No one can tell what they were like" (*Antiquities of the Jews* 8.3.3). However, even though the Israelite design may have been unique in form, the shared elements in design throughout the ancient Near East reflect an original source that influenced both Israelite and pagan style. J.M.P. Otts explains this:

> It has been thought by some that Moses caught the idea of the ark and the cherubim from the Egyptians, and that they in turn had caught the idea from the Babylonians and Persians. But there was, no doubt, a *protevangelium* [first proclamation of the Gospel, Genesis 3:15] preached at the gate of paradise; and a typical form of worship was then instituted, which was the common mode among men before the flood, and which prevailed up to the dispersion of families after the flood; and so we are not to be surprised at finding many religious symbols in pagan worship similar to those that were in use among the ancient Jews; and the fact that sacred chests or cistae similar to the Mosaic ark, and many figures of composite beings with wings and faces similar to cherubim, are found to have been common in the worship of all eastern nations, does not argue that Moses derived his ideas from Egypt or any other pagan source, but rather that traditions and reminiscences of the protevangel and the primitive forms of worship have been carried into

> all nations of the earth, but were more fully conserved in some than in others.[9]

That Israel adopted practices identical with other pagan cultures does not challenge God's unique revelation to them as the chosen people. Some explain this by showing the reasonableness of God using local customs—but with a distinct theological meaning—that magnified the God of Israel by contrast.

Has Archaeology Found the Place of the Ark?

According to ancient sources such as Josephus and the Mishnah tractate *Middot,* the Ark once rested on a bedrock platform called in Jewish tradition *'Even Ha-Shetiyah* ("the Foundation Stone") and in Arabic *es-Sakhra* ("the Rock"). According to Leen Ritmeyer, former Chief Architect of the Temple Mount excavations under Benjamin Mazar and today Director of Ritmeyer Archaeological Design in England, the huge rock within the present-day Islamic Dome of the Rock is the bedrock platform within the Holy of Holies.[10]

Ritmeyer attributed cuts in the platform in the north, south, and west to the action of the Crusaders in 1099 when they turned the structure into a place of Christian worship called the *Templum Domini.* The Crusaders thought that the rock disfigured the Temple of the Lord and so shaped it into a more acceptable size and built an altar on top of it. In 1187, when the caliph Saladin recaptured the Dome of the Rock, he found the rock covered with marble slabs. Once he had removed the slabs, he found that the platform had been mutilated. This mutilation included the cave and deep tunneling beneath the platform, which may have been attempts by the Crusaders to locate the Ark. The natural cave below the platform was identified by the Crusader period as

Bedrock inside the Islamic Dome of the Rock where the Ark once rested in the Holy of Holies. Photo by Paul Streber.

the Holy of Holies. There the Crusaders commemorated the visitation of the angel to Zacharias. They enlarged the cave in order to use it as a sanctuary. They burned candles and incense in the cave, requiring a vertical shaft for ventilation (the present hole in the rock).

Having identified these structures, Ritmeyer began looking for additional clues to position the Holy of Holies on the rock. He tells the story of his insight for this identification:

> While flying to Israel, 30,000 feet high in the air, I got my first glimpse of the most spectacular of all the discoveries, namely that of the former location of the Ark of the Covenant! Averting my gaze from the in-flight video, I took out a large photograph of the Sakhra from my briefcase and tried to trace again those flat areas, which of course, were familiar to me as foundation trenches.... I also drew a dotted line where the Veil, which separated the Holy of Holies from the Holy, would have hung. I did not expect to find any remains there as no wall existed there. I then suddenly noticed in the middle of this square a dark rectangle! What could it be? The first thing that came to mind was, of course, the Ark of the Covenant, which once stood in the centre of the Holy of Holies in Solomon's Temple. But that surely could not be true, I thought.... [However,] according to my plan, it falls exactly in the centre of the Holy of Holies. The dimensions of this level basin agree with those of the Ark of the Covenant which were 1.5 x 2.5 cubits (2'7" x 4'4" or 79 cm. x 131 cm.), with the longitudinal axis coinciding with that of the Temple. Its location is rather unique, as it could only have been the place where the Ark of the Covenant once stood. It is clear that without such a flat area the Ark would have wobbled about in an undignified manner, which would not conceivably have been allowed.[11]

This depression, according to Ritmeyer, must have served as a base to secure the Ark within the Holy of Holies. It could not have been a creation of the Crusaders because they covered the rock platform with slabs to hide it.[12] Archaeological investigation of the area to confirm Ritmeyer's conclusions is presently impossible due to the strict control of the area by the Islamic authorities. But if he is correct, the site of the Holy of Holies and the former location of the Ark of the Covenant has now been identified.

The parallels to the Ark in the ancient Near East that we have seen have led some people to suggest that the Israelites either borrowed or shared the region's mythology. However, the biblical account demonstrates the theological uniqueness of the Ark with respect to other cultures. For this evidence we need to search through the history of the relationship between Israel and the Ark.

4
Israel and the Ark

Jerusalem is in the center of the world,
the Temple Mount is in the center of Jerusalem,
the Temple is in the center of the Temple Mount, the
Holy of Holies is in the center of the Temple,
and the Ark is in the center of the Holy of Holies.

—MIDRASH TANHUMA, *KEDOSHIM 10*

None of Israel's treasures has ever held the preeminent place of the Ark. It alone contained the great covenant of Moses made at Sinai. It alone once hosted the great glory of God. What could compare with the Ark? However, with the destruction of the First Temple more than 2500 years ago, the Ark of the Covenant disappeared from the biblical record. Ever since, men have sought to solve the secret of the lost Ark. To find it would undoubtedly be the greatest archaeological, historical, religious, and political discovery of all time! As Talmudic scholar Rabbi Leibel Reznick wrote, "No other archaeological find would have a greater impact on the destiny of man. What a religious resurgence [this] discovery would cause. How it would cause scholars and laymen to reevaluate the past, examine the present, and speculate on the future cannot be imagined."[1]

Yet the search for such a treasure of the past must begin in the present by learning its history. Such a history is surely essential for understanding Israel's ancient religious institutions, including the Temple and its services. For Christians, this also offers a rich analogy of the work of Jesus as Savior and High Priest. Without such background, a book like the New Testament letter to the Hebrews would be largely unintelligible.

The Ark and the Conquest

At the conclusion of the exodus came the wilderness wandering and the beginning of the conquest. Before Israel lay the unconquered Land given to Abraham by the God who had made and possessed it all. Constituted as a nation at Sinai, now the people would begin to function as a nation. They needed only a homeland. In the battle to possess the Land, the Ark was at the forefront, assuring these untrained warriors that God would go before them and win the victory, for "the battle is the LORD'S" (1 Samuel 17:47).

Recreation of Kohathites transporting the Ark into battle.
Photo courtesy of Desperado Films, Sun International Pictures.

As the Ark traveled and camped with the Israelites, its usual position was in the middle of the assembled tribes (Numbers 2:17; 10:14-28). This was to remind Israel that God was fulfilling His promise to dwell in their midst. Joshua 3:3-4 tells us that at the first crossing of the Jordan, the Ark was repositioned at the head of the tribes, and all Israel was commanded to follow it. The reason given in the text is "that you may know the way by which you shall go, for you have not passed this way before."

Thus, the Ark provided both divine guidance and powerful protection for the Israelites. It served as a focus for their faith in an unknown and untried place. God was not to be in the background of their lives but always in the forefront—the One who must be followed by faith when passing through the deep waters of life.

To confirm this truth, the Ark divided the waters of the Jordan just as the Red Sea had parted at the crossing of these Israelites' ancestors (Joshua 3:14-17; see Exodus 14:21-22). The Jordan was at that season overflowing its banks, and the waters were stopped as far as 15 miles upstream (verses 15-16), so this was indeed a miracle comparable to that performed at the Red Sea.

The Ark led the way before the Israelite army at Jericho, bringing down its walls as the seventh trumpet blast on the seven trumpets on the seventh day announced the presence of the God of all creation (Joshua 6:4-20). Through this encounter, and others to come, Israel learned that to fight without the Ark of God meant sure defeat—a lesson their faithless forefathers never learned (Numbers 14:44-45). After learning a similar lesson of obedience at Ai (Joshua 7–8:29), the nation renewed its loyalty to the Mosaic covenant at Joshua's altar. The Ark was placed between the tribes in the valley that divided the twin mountains Ebal and Gerazim (Joshua 8:30-35).

Even though the Ark reminded Israel of the lessons they learned during the conquest, when they were at rest in the Land, the people apparently forgot about the Ark. For over 100 years it remained at Shiloh and at other sites until King David restored its central status by installing it at Jerusalem. The Ark appeared in history at Israel's first entrance into the Land as a nation, and it disappeared at Israel's first exit as a nation. The first event was accompanied by Israel's faith, and thus they conquered. In the last event, Israel had lost their faith, and thus they were conquered. The hinge of history truly swung upon the Ark.

The Ark and the Judges

In the distressing days of the Judges, when "everyone did what was right in his own eyes" (Judges 21:25), another turning point occurred in Israel's history. They transitioned from a theocracy, in which God ruled the nation directly through His spiritual representatives, to a monarchy, in which God ruled indirectly through a political representative, the king. The Ark was a part of this great period of transition as well.

In 1 Samuel 6–7 we have the account of the capture of the Ark. As we have already pointed out, this was the result of misplaced faith on the part of the Israelites. God is a jealous God (Exodus 20:5; Deuteronomy 6:15) and will brook no rivals—even His own Ark, which the desperate people transformed into a magic talisman (1 Samuel 4:3). God called Israel to be a light to the Gentile nations, a witness of the true God. This witness, which involved a demonstration of God's superiority and sovereignty, was only possible in the context of holiness and obedience to God's laws.

In 1 Samuel 2:12–3:18, the loss of Israel's holiness and obedience preceded the loss of the Ark. The capture of the Ark followed the capture of the hearts of the high priest and his priestly sons to overindulgence (2:13-16; see 4:18), apathy (2:23-25; 3:13), unbridled lust (2:22), and spiritual rebellion (2:12,25). Furthermore, the beginning of this account tells us that "word from the LORD was rare in those days" (3:1). The theocracy had failed because God's rule was not evident in His own priests, who were to rule over His nation. God therefore rejected the high priest Eli's line with this famous admonition: "For those who honor Me I will honor, and those who despise Me will be lightly esteemed" (2:30). Israel could not follow Samuel's worthless sons, and so they rebelled against God's direct rule and asked for a king like the other nations (1 Samuel 8:3-5).

Israel had turned the Ark into a sort of fetish. As a result, God could not use the Ark to demonstrate His sovereignty through Israel. Therefore, to show Israel they had abandoned God by asking for a king (1 Samuel 8:7), and to carry on the mission of witness before the nations, God permitted the Philistines to capture the Ark. The departure of Eli parallels the departure of the Ark as news of its loss costs him his life (4:18). A literary connection seems to exist between Eli's fall from his throne (1 Samuel 1:9; 4:13,18) and the fall of God's throne (the cherubim with the Ark) to the enemy. God did not leave His people, but His people left Him. We see this drama of departure in full relief as Eli's daughter-in-law, distressed at her family's deaths and the Ark's capture, gives birth prematurely and names the child Ichabod, meaning "the glory [the Ark] has departed" (4:19-21).

For the Philistines, the arrival of the Ark was the arrival of defeat. When they placed the Ark in the pagan temples to defile it, it defiled those temples instead. Thus the Philistines learned what they had previously feared (4:8): No god could stand before the Ark (5:1-5). In addition, these enemies of God could not escape the plagues that befell them in every city the Ark visited (5:6-12). Their punishment was similar to that of the Egyptians, who had likewise defied God and His people, Israel.

When the Philistines returned the Ark to Israel, they were a fearful adversary. The restoration of the Ark was therefore a testimony of divine sovereignty (6:1-3,7-12). It also came bearing gifts of appeasement to the Israelites (6:8,15-18), who unfortunately had not yet learned the lessons their enemies had painfully acquired.

As soon as the Ark reached the border of Israel at Beth-shemesh, a number of the men lined up to take turns peering into it.[2] Consequently, all these men died. First Samuel 6:20 expresses the great fear of all Israel: "Who is able to stand before the LORD, this holy God? And to whom shall He go up from us?" Rather than repent and draw near to God, these people wanted to put God as far away from them as possible.

We see Israel's attitude toward the Ark continued in their first king, Saul. He was chosen by human standards, a head above the rest (literally—1 Samuel 9:2). First Chronicles 13:1-3 reports the later assessment by Israel's leaders: "Let us bring back the ark of our God to us, for we did not seek it in the days of Saul."

The Ark and King David

The great transition during this period is from the rule of Saul to that of David, whose heart was in tune with God's (1 Samuel 13:14). David's first concern was the conquest of Jerusalem, which enabled the fulfillment of the age-old promise of God to settle His people and His presence (Exodus 15:17; 25:8; 2 Samuel 7:10,13). Then, David's thoughts immediately turned to the Ark. His desire was to build a Temple, which, like the Tabernacle, would be designed for the single purpose of housing the

Ark (2 Samuel 7:1-2; Psalm 132:4-5; see 1 Chronicles 22:19; 28:2). His spiritual insight concerning the need for a permanent home for the Ark, around which all of Israel could center their lives, was apparently drawn from deep meditation on Scripture and on his experiences (see Psalm 132). This insight and desire to house the Ark was lost for a time when David lapsed into sin (2 Samuel 11). On that occasion, when David was in the midst of an affair with Bathsheba, God used her husband to show David his decline. Ironically, when David attempted to get Uriah to sleep with his wife to cover his own adultery, this resident Gentile declared that he would not go up to his house while the Ark remained in a tent (verse 11).

At Kiriath-jearim, where the Ark had been brought after the disaster at Beth-shemesh, a qualified priest and his three sons, Abinadab, Eleazer, Uzzah, and Ahio, properly attended it. The transportation of the Ark from Kiriath-jearim to Jerusalem in the same manner as it had been brought—by oxcart—was not according to God's specific instruction to the Levites (Exodus 37:5; 1 Chronicles 15:15). Only the Kohathites were to transport the Ark—by its poles and on their shoulders (Exodus 25:14-15; Numbers 3:30-31; 4:15; 7:9). Whether David understood this or not is uncertain, but the death of the priest's son Uzzah for touching the Ark was a result of this violation. God may have delayed the transfer of the Ark in order to teach Israel that the final decision for its location was with God and not with man.[3] Even David could not dictate the movement of the Ark—it could only come to Jerusalem by the will of God. After the death of Uzzah, David left the Ark in the charge of a Philistine named Obed-edom (2 Samuel 6:10). The fact that it did not destroy his house, as it had when it previously stayed in Philistine homes (1 Samuel 5:6-12), was confirmation to David that the direction toward Jerusalem was the direction of blessing (2 Samuel 6:11-12).

The Ark and Jerusalem

David illustrates the change from Saul's self-centered administration to his own spiritual administration by personally donning the priestly ephod and escorting the Ark to Jerusalem in joyous celebration (2 Samuel 6:14). When Saul sought to take the place of the priest, the Lord removed the kingdom from him (1 Samuel 13:8-14), but after David did it, God promised to establish his kingdom forever (2 Samuel 7:16). The difference is in their hearts. Saul explained that he "forced himself" to act (1 Samuel 13:12), whereas David did it willingly, even at the cost of being misunderstood and maligned (2 Samuel 6:20-21; 1 Chronicles 15:29). Saul had no concern for proper procedure or for God's commandments (1 Samuel 13:13), but David was careful to obey the law of the Ark (1 Chronicles 15:2,12-15) and to do what he did "before the LORD" (2 Samuel 6:21; see 1 Chronicles 16:29). Further, Saul had usurped the priestly prerogative, but David had joined with the priest (1 Chronicles 15:25-27).

Scholars have found in documents from the ancient Near East a possible explanation for the contrast between Saul's actions and David's actions concerning the Ark. The royal inscriptions of Mesopotamia portray the legitimate king as the restorer of the forgotten "cult." Psalm 132 depicts David in this same light. The psalmist is writing about a procession of the Ark. He records David's vow to not rest until the Ark is restored to prominence. He cites 2 Chronicles 6:41, a reference to the installation of the Ark in the Temple, which is connected to David's faithfulness. Thus, the Ark was central to the recognition and establishment of a king "after God's own heart."

For this reason scholars have also seen David's bringing of the Ark to Jerusalem as a climactic new exodus. The captivity of the Ark in Philistia paralleled the captivity of Israel in Egypt. The miraculous actions of the Ark among the Philistines paralleled God's miracles in Egypt. And the Ark entered into Jerusalem as "their own place" (2 Samuel 7:10; 1 Chronicles 17:9) just as Israel entered into Canaan, the Promised Land.

The Ark and King Solomon

God was making a new beginning with His people in Jerusalem as He had at the exodus. This was demonstrated as Solomon constructed the Temple and brought the Ark into it (1 Chronicles 22:19; 2 Chronicles 3:1; 5:4-7; 6:10-11). Solomon's dedication of the Temple was the high point of his spiritual career and a major turning point in Israel's history. For the first time, the nation was at peace on every side, the kingdoms of Israel and Judah were consolidated and unified with Jerusalem as their capital (see Ezekiel 5:5), and the Ark had ceased its wanderings among the tribes to take its home in the Temple (2 Samuel 7:6; Psalm 132:13-14). To connect the Temple with the Tabernacle and provide a continuity from the days of the exodus to that day, God's glory returned to take its place between the wings of the cherubim (1 Kings 8:10-11; 2 Chronicles 5:13-14; 7:1-3).

Once the Ark was attached to the Temple it was to remain there, and people were to pray in its direction from every place on earth (1 Kings 8:30,41-43; 2 Chronicles 6:20). This explains the absence of the Ark in military engagements after the time of Solomon.[4] Now, in times of war, the Ark would not need to go to the battlefield. From the battlefield, soldiers would direct their prayers toward the Ark (1 Kings 8:44-45). If they were suffering defeat, they should understand the problem was their sin, and they should come to the Ark with their penitent supplications (2 Chronicles 6:24-25). The Psalms may reflect that the Ark made annual processions to the Mount of Olives to reassure Israel of God's presence and to renew loyalty to the covenant (see Psalm 24; 47; 68; 132). This may be why the glory later departed along this route before the Temple's destruction (Ezekiel 11:23). Nevertheless, the Ark, like the nation, seemed to experience a time of rest during the days of Solomon and for a short time thereafter. But things were about to change again.

The Ark and the Apostasy

The final turn of Israelite history upon the hinge of the Ark comes during the great civil war, which divided the kingdom between the north (Israel) and the south (Judah). This war moved the Temple toward destruction and the nation toward exile. King Solomon's compromise with his foreign wives' religions put the nation on the path of spiritual defection and decline (1 Kings 11:1-28). The prophet Ahijah had predicted that this sin started a process that would ultimately tear the kingdom in two (1 Kings 11:29-35). When the kingdom of Israel did secede from Judah, it lost access to the Lord's presence at the Ark in Jerusalem, which was in Judah (1 Kings 12:27).

To satisfy Israel's need for a sanctuary, Jeroboam constructed alternate worship sites at Dan and Bethel, the northern and southern borders of the kingdom (1 Kings 12:28-29). Because the Ark was only in the Judean Temple, Jeroboam substituted a rival to the Ark at each of his new religious centers. He reasoned that since the Ark had come from Sinai, a place associated with the covenant and Israelite origins, he needed another religious symbol also from this same site. Therefore he chose the symbol of the golden calf (1 Kings 12:28), which had been made by the high priest Aaron and associated with the worship of the true God (Exodus 32:1-6). This appeared to be a smart religious and political move because to the uninformed Israelite, this symbol had the authority of the Aaronic priesthood and was part of the exodus tradition. At the calves' dedication he even used the same injunction that Aaron had pronounced (1 Kings 12:28). By this action the Israelites obtained access to a historical sanctuary, but they also inherited the history of corruption and judgment that was part and parcel of it (see Exodus 32:8-10). At Sinai the people had Moses to intercede and save them from total annihilation (Exodus 32:11-35). This time, however, Israel had no one to appease God's wrath, for that was only possible through legitimate priests officiating at the Ark (Leviticus 16:29-34). Consequently, the Assyrians exiled the Israelites, leaving only the southern kingdom of Judah.

But the apostasy had begun in Judah. After the demise of Israel in the north, the apostasy returned to Judah to inflict a greater desecration than Israel had ever known. The apex of this apostasy came with the reign of King Manasseh, who renovated the sanctuary according to a pagan design. He apparently did this by removing all the Temple vessels and replacing them with pagan idols, which the biblical text refers to as "the abominations of the nations" (2 Kings 21:2-7; 2 Chronicles 33:2-7). The text implies that in place of the Ark he put an image of the Canaanite fertility goddess Asherah (2 Kings 21:7; 2 Chronicles 33:7). We don't know what happened to the Ark in th time of Manasseh, but when we come to the time of Manasseh's grandson, Josiah, we find the Ark still in existence (2 Chronicles 35:3).

The Ark at the End of an Era

Josiah was a godly king who sought to make spiritual and political reforms based on the Torah. He began by renovating and purifying the Temple, which Manasseh had desecrated (2 Chronicles 34:8-33). As part of this necessary reform, he ordered the Ark returned to the Temple by the faithful Levites, whose job was to transport it whenever it had to be moved (2 Chronicles 35:3). Despite the good start begun with the reforms of Josiah, his era experienced a bitter end. Josiah unwisely went to engage in battle the Egyptian pharaoh Neco, who had crossed his realm at the Megiddo Pass to join the Assyrians in war against the Babylonians (2 Kings 23:29). Josiah was killed, and his death precipitated a rapid political and spiritual decline in Israel (2 Chronicles 25:20-24). Egypt imposed hegemony over Judah, whose two successive rulers were evil, leading in little more than a decade to an invasion by the Babylonians (2 Chronicles 36:1-10) and the end of the Israelite monarchy. Manasseh's sin, which was blamed for Judah's fall, brought with it the fall of Jerusalem and the loss of the Temple with all it contained.

The Disappearance of the Ark

After the exile, a Jewish remnant returned to Judah and rebuilt the Temple. However, Jewish historical sources are united in affirming that the Ark did not return with the exiles and was not present in the Holy of Holies in the Second Temple. The prophets Isaiah and Jeremiah record the loss of the Temple treasures, chief of which was the Ark: "Our holy and beautiful house, where our fathers praised You, has been burned by fire; and all our precious things have become a ruin" (Isaiah 64:11). "In the days of her affliction and homelessness Jerusalem remembers all her precious things that were from the days of old.... The adversary has stretched out his hand over all her precious things, for she has seen the nations enter her sanctuary" (Lamentations 1:7,10). Rather than explaining the disappearance of the Ark, Jeremiah attempts to console the people in their grief over its loss by predicting a future restoration: "'It shall be in those days when you are multiplied and increased in the land,' declares the LORD, 'they no longer will say "The ark of the covenant of the LORD." And it shall not come to mind, nor will they remember it, nor will they miss it, nor will it be made again'" (Jeremiah 3:16).

These verses reveal the biblical verdict that the Ark disappeared with the destruction of the Temple in 586 B.C. Yet every reader of this biblical account still wonders, *What happened to the Ark?* Why does the biblical text remain silent concerning such a monumental event? Given the rich history of the Ark and its pivotal role in Israel's own history, how can it have vanished from the sacred page without a word? The most important object in the world, in the biblical view, simply ceases to be in the story. As Professor Richard E. Friedman declared, "There is no report that the Ark was carried away or destroyed or hidden."[5] There is not even any comment such as "And then the Ark disappeared, and we do not know what happened to it" or "And no one knows where it is to this day." How could Israel's greatest treasure, the center of its national worship, the very reason for the Temple's existence, and, above all, the place of God's presence, vanish into the dust of time without a trace? According to Hebrew University professor Menahem Haran, "Its disappearance is one of the enigmas in the history of the First Temple."[6]

Curiously, the Bible carefully tracks other Temple items less precious by comparison that also disappeared with the Temple's destruction. If the text appears deliberately silent concerning the disappearance of the Ark, can we hope to know what happened to it? In order to find the answer we must ask the Bible four questions. Join me in the next chapter as we begin our search for the Ark.

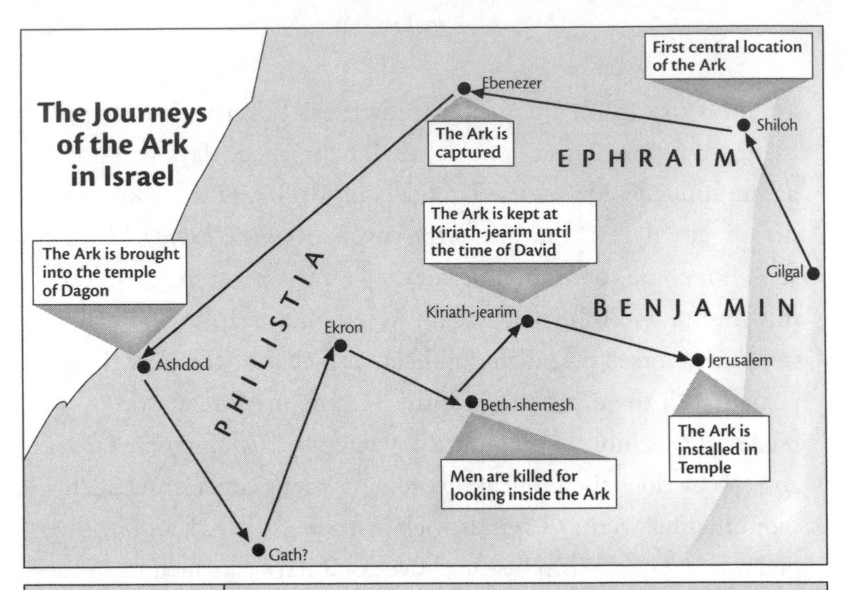

	History of the Ark
c. 1446 B.C.	Moses' craftsman Bezalel constructs the Ark
c. 1406 B.C.	The Ark crosses the Jordan River ahead of the Israelites
c. 1406 B.C.	The Ark leads the army of Israel in its march around the walls of Jericho
c. 1400 B.C.	The Ark is set between Mount Ebal and Gerazim
c. 1399–1385 B.C.	The Ark is stationed with the Tabernacle at Gilgal
c. 1385–1050 B.C.	The Ark is housed with the Tabernacle at Shiloh
c. 1050 B.C.	The Ark is captured by the Philistines
c. 1049 B.C.	The Ark miraculously is carried into Israelite territory of Beth-shemesh on a cart
c. 1048–1028 B.C.	The Ark is transferred to Kiriath-jearim
c. 999 B.C.	David transfers the Ark to Jerusalem
950 B.C.	Solomon installs the Ark with the Tabernacle and other Temple vessels in the First Temple
701 B.C.	King Hezekiah lays the letter of the Assyrian Rabshakeh before the Ark
695–642 B.C.	King Manasseh places idols within the Holy Place and the Holy of Holies. Faithful Levites remove the Ark
622 B.C.	King Josiah commands the Levites to return the Ark to the restored Temple
605 B.C.	According to tradition, the Ark and the Temple treasures are placed under the Temple Mount

PART 2

Searching for the Location of the Ark

5
What Happened to the Ark?

TOP SECRET
ARMY INTEL #9906753
DO NOT OPEN

According to the popular film *Raiders of the Lost Ark*, the final disposition of the Ark was an old government warehouse filled with thousands of identical crates left to gather dust. In this fiction, only someone who happened to discover this warehouse and who cared to search for the Ark in this endless sea of boxes would find it under the label TOP SECRET. ARMY INTEL #9906753. DO NOT OPEN.

Likewise, in the world of fact, anyone who would search for the Ark must first care to search for it among the seemingly endless theories proposed by researchers. Unfortunately, no secret label can help with this search. We must begin by asking the right questions if we are to discover an answer to what happened to the Ark: Was it captured? Was it destroyed? Or was it placed in hiding and lost? Between the Old Testament book of Malachi and the New Testament book of Matthew are four hundred years of silence. Apocryphal accounts such as those in 2 Esdras and Talmud Babli attempt to fill in the gap with stories of the Ark's capture. However, since 2 Esdras was written 600 years later, and the Talmud was not completed for another 200 to 600 years, these stories are mere speculation. And if the Ark was captured, how could the Jews, who so revered it, leave no record of their lament over its loss or expectation of its recovery?

In this chapter we will attempt to read between the lines of history and Scripture and determine whether the Bible is as silent as people have assumed. Perhaps in weighing the available evidence of the text, we will be able to move closer to answering the age-old question, What happened to the Ark?

The Bible only gives a hint of what may have happened to the Temple treasures. To fill out the picture we need other hints that permit us to form reasonable theories of their location. We have such hints preserved in extrabiblical documents that span a 400-year period often called "the silent years." Four centuries did in fact elapse between the last book of the Old Testament and the coming of Jesus, but these were anything but silent. During this time much important and formative history passed for the Jewish nation. Also, a rich heritage of tradition and prophetic development filled these years. The result was an extensive collection of legends and traditions that are clearly in a different category from the inspired Scriptures. With careful use, however, they can reveal significant pieces of past history and religious practice. "Uninspired" does not mean "unimportant." Any writing that comes to us from the time or near the time of the Bible is of immense value. It may give us eyewitness reports of events not covered in Scripture or provide our only source for the experiences of daily life during times now forgotten. Who is not aware of the great contribution to biblical understanding that has come to us from writings such as those of the first-century Jewish historian Josephus and the Dead Sea Scrolls, written before and during the life of Jesus? These, and a whole library of texts known as the Apocrypha and Pseudepigrapha, offer information concerning both the Temple treasures and the end times.

To these we must add the vast storehouse of learning contained in the Jewish Talmud and the many commentaries by rabbis on the Bible. Christian scholars are now aware that these sources have long held vital insights about life and religion in both the Old and New Testaments. They have helped resolve many unanswered questions concerning biblical and historical interpretations, and they have given us a much clearer picture of the life of Jesus as a Jew. Since they were written to preserve and explain Jewish law in the Bible and practical laws that flow from these, they carefully describe laws about the Temple and its treasures. The judicious use of these works to clarify and confirm New Testament truths should be acceptable to concerned Christians. In fact, the study of the earliest history of the church reveals that Christian scholars used these works.

Historians and archaeologists once generally assumed that the story of the Ark came to an end sometime during the period of the monarchy because the Bible does not mention it thereafter. One statement from a record composed after the exile implies the Ark was present "to this day" (2 Chronicles 5:9). The Gemara in *Yoma* 53b says that a dispute arose between Rabbi Eliezer and Rabbi Simeon ben Yohai on the one hand, and Rabbi Judah ben Il'ai on the other. The former contended that the Ark had gone into exile in Babylon (citing 2 Chronicles 36:10; Isaiah 39:6; Lamentations 1:6). The latter held that the Ark was buried in its own place (citing 1 Kings 8:8). Rabbi Judah had used the phrase in 1 Kings 8:8 "They are there to this day," concerning the appearance of the Ark's poles sticking out of the Holy of Holies, to mean "forever." The other rabbis disproved this meaning to the phrase and thus won the argument.

In agreement with the "winning" rabbis, a similar reference in 2 Chronicles 5:9 most likely refers to an earlier time when the

Temple was standing (a hundred years before). It is apparently taken from the parallel passage in 1 Kings 8:8, which Rabbi Judah had used for his support. But the same argument applies: "Unto this day" means "the day of the Temple."

As the above dispute reveals, a number of historical proposals tried to account for what happened to the Ark. Let us consider several explanations that have been offered from the biblical text for the time of the Ark's disappearance.

The Attack of Pharaoh Shishak

Shortly after the death of Solomon and the division of the kingdom under his son Rehoboam (circa 926 B.C.), the Egyptian pharaoh Sheshonk I (Shishak) invaded the weakened southern kingdom of Judah. The biblical text states quite clearly that he "came up against Jerusalem" and that he "took away the treasures of the house of the LORD" (1 Kings 14:25-26).

The temple of Karnak in Luxor, Egypt, contains Shishak's own account of his triumph. There we learn that he presented the spoils of his Palestinian campaign as a dedicatory offering to his patron god, Amun. In addition, when Shishak's tomb was discovered in Tanis in 1939, both his sarcophagus and his mummy were lavishly adorned with gold. Perhaps the source of some of this gold was Solomon's Temple, since his plunder from there included 500 shields of beaten gold (1 Kings 10:16-17). On this basis, some scholars have thought that this provides evidence of the Ark being taken, presented to Amun, and then perhaps melted down to be recast for royal use. This theory received popular exposure when Spielberg and Lucas adopted it for their explanation of the Ark's location in their first Indiana Jones film. This theory has significant difficulties, however.

First, neither the Bible nor extrabiblical texts report that Shishak even entered Jerusalem! Shishak's own record of the 156 cities he captured did not include the mention of Jerusalem. The statements in 1 Kings 14:25-26 that he "came against Jerusalem" and "took away the treasures of the house of the LORD" may only mean that he exacted tribute from the city.[1] King Jeroboam would have willingly paid this tribute because he owed Shishak a debt for granting him political asylum when his father, Solomon, sought to assassinate him (1 Kings 11:34-35,40).

Second, the tribute was "the treasures of the house of the LORD and the treasures of the king's house" (1 Kings 14:26). These were the items stored in the Temple treasury outside the Temple proper and in part of the palace complex called the House of Lebanon (1 Kings 7:1-12; 10:17). Based on the repeated association of the treasuries to the king's house in the Bible, we may assume that these storehouses were similar in nature. The text does not list which specific vessels were taken, so his spoil probably only consisted of non-ritual objects or of vessels not in present use in the Temple service. First Kings 7:51 tells us that these treasuries included the spoils of war taken from defeated enemies (see 2 Samuel 8:7-12). This treasure was certainly valuable, and it was dedicated to the Lord, but it did not at all compare with the sanctity of the Temple vessels and especially the Ark. What was plundered was stated specifically in 1 Kings 14:26 (see 2 Chronicles 12:9) in Hebrew as *'otzarot beit hamelech* ("the royal storehouses"). The treasure that Shishak took was from these storehouses of gold and silver that were used to finance the Temple budget and that also housed the national treasures. Although the account says that he took "everything," it does not state that he entered the Temple itself or that he took any of the holy vessels. The "everything" therefore probably includes all of the nation's major monetary assets. The text does, however, specify one set of gold items, Solomon's golden shields. From this mention of one set of gold vessels, we can deduce that this was the most significant item captured, certainly a treasure far inferior to that of the holy vessels and especially the Ark.

Third, if Shishak had taken all of the Temple treasures, then how is it that the text reveals shortly after the invasion such vessels as the altar of incense, the menorah, and the table of showbread still in use in the Temple (2 Chronicles 13:11)? These probably could not have been newly constructed because the only items expressly said to have been remade are the shields (this time of brass—1 Kings 14:27). Since the Ark is not a "repeatable" item, if it had been taken, it could not reappear later in the text. However, we read that as late as the time of Josiah it was still in existence (2 Chronicles 35:3).

Because of this contrary evidence, the Egyptian theory of disappearance fails. With it, for similar reasons, we may put to rest the theory that the Ark was later taken by King Jehoash of Israel in his battle against Judah in 785 B.C. (2 Kings 14:14) or by King Hezekiah of Judah in 729 B.C. as tribute payment to the Assyrians (2 Kings 18:15-16). In the case of Jehoash, his was not an invasion to capture the Temple treasure, but a forced encounter that he joined to teach a lesson to Amaziah, king of Judah (2 Chronicles 25:17-24). He did take "gold and silver and all the utensils" from "the house of God," but not from the Temple proper. They were from the house of Obed-edom, whose family served as gatekeepers (verse 24; see 1 Chronicles 26:4-8).

In the case of Hezekiah, the text makes it clear that he went "before the LORD...enthroned above the cherubim" (that is, "before the Ark") to pray for Jerusalem's deliverance from the Assyrian siege (2 Kings 19:14-15). However, this was the only access the king would have been permitted. He could never have entered the Holy of Holies itself. When King Uzziah (Hezekiah's great-grandfather) had entered only the outer division of the Temple to burn incense on the golden Altar, he was struck with leprosy till his death (2 Chronicles 26:16-21).

This evidence forced scholar Herbert May to this conclusion:

> That the Jerusalem ark still existed at the time of Josiah [circa 621 B.C.] is hardly to be doubted. The fact that it is not mentioned in the account of the sack of the Temple in 586 B.C. is insufficient reason for assuming that it must have disappeared earlier at the time when Shishak sacked the Temple of its treasures in the reign of Rehoboam, or when the wealth of the Temple was seized at the time of Asa and Ben-Hadad [1 Kings 15:18], or Amaziah and Jehoahaz [2 Kings 14:14], or Ahaz and Tiglath-Pileser [2 Kings 16:8].[2]

The Desecration of King Manasseh

Another theory for the Ark's disappearance from the Temple is that the Ark was removed by the evil Judean king Manasseh when he desecrated the Temple by turning it into a center for pagan shrines (2 Kings 21:7; 2 Chronicles 33:7). Previous kings had placed images of idols outside the city (1 Kings 11:7; 15:13; 16:32-33) and even inside the city but always outside of the Temple precinct (2 Kings 11:18). Manasseh performed the ultimate act of desecration by placing his idols "in the two courts of the house of the LORD" (2 Kings 21:4-5), but beyond this, within the house of the Lord itself (verse 7). Some scholars believe that he went so far as to actually place a pagan image within the Holy of Holies, because verse 7 adds the phrase "[the place where] I will put My name forever." But the text does not state that this refers specifically to the Holy of Holies—only to "this house" and to "Jerusalem."

However, Menachem Haran argues on the basis of the arrangement of pagan worship shrines in the ancient Near East that the image of Asherah must have been installed in the Holy of Holies. Since Manasseh had already placed vessels for Baal and Asherah in the outer division of the Temple, the fitting place for the image of the goddess was within the inner division. Furthermore, when 50 years later Josiah removes this image as part of his reforms, the text indicates that the Ark had not been in the Holy of Holies (2 Kings 23:6; 2 Chronicles 35:3). Haran therefore assumes that Manasseh would have destroyed the Ark and other Temple vessels in order to accomplish this replacement of the deity and her attendants. The evidence to the contrary is not as impressive as that against the previous theories, but we must consider some other factors.

Whether or not Manasseh actually entered the innermost sanctuary, this act represented the first time in history that the Temple ceased to function because of desecration. Therefore, for all practical purposes, the function of the Ark was removed, if not the Ark itself. Our main problem with this theory is that the text does not say that Manasseh destroyed any of these vessels, only that he put others in their place. Further, Manasseh was not attempting to remove God from the Temple but to incorporate Canannite religion into the traditional religion.

What Manasseh was doing—making changes in religion—is called syncretism. This is a merging or substitution of the elements of another religion (in this case the popular religion of those living with and around the Israelites) while making claim to the original religion. It is the same thing Jeroboam did when he installed the golden calves at Dan and Bethel in place of the Ark at Jerusalem. In his view, he was still true to the Israelite God. He was just using different symbols for Him. Let us be clear that God hates this kind of thinking. He considers it idolatry and false worship. Nevertheless, the Ark was not simply a part of Israel's religion but was an essential part of Israel's constitutional and political existence. The tablets of the law were foundational to the nation, and Jeroboam, whatever he might have done with lesser vessels, could not easily overlook this fact about the Ark.

Perhaps Manasseh's later reforming actions, after his repentance (2 Chronicles 33:11-16), can provide some clues to his former conduct with the Temple vessels. His return to the Lord came only after he was captured and tortured by the Babylonians. Some people come to God when they see the light—others only when they feel the heat! So when Manasseh got really "heated" (or as the text says, "in distress"), he cried out to God for release and God restored him to his throne. "Then Manasseh knew that the LORD was God" (verses 12-13).

His return to the true faith meant he had to dispose of the false religion, so we read that he had his idols and cultic implements removed from the Temple and thrown outside the city (verse 15). This does not mean that Manasseh destroyed them but only that he moved them outside of the city, as had been the norm for previous kings who set up pagan worship centers. Manasseh was like many who change their ways after they have gone far in sin. They consider themselves to have fully repented, but others think they still have a long way to go. That Manasseh did not destroy his own idols is evident from the fact that his son and heir, Amon, restored the false worship and "sacrificed to all the carved images which his father Manasseh had made" (2 Chronicles 33:22).

So Manasseh could not bring himself to destroy his pagan idols even after he repented. How can we expect him to have earlier destroyed the most sacred and important item in all of Israel, the Ark? I believe that the answer will be that Manasseh could not have removed or destroyed the Ark because it had already been put beyond his reach by the Levites. This is implied by 2 Chronicles 35:3, which records these priests later returning the Ark to the purified Temple. But that is a story for the next chapter.

The Babylonian Invasion

Most scholars believe the Ark met its end during the Babylonian invasion of Jerusalem between 605 and 586 B.C. Two variations on the final disposition of the Ark spring from this theory. Some suppose that the Babylonians removed the Ark from the Temple along with other Temple vessels when they looted the Temple treasuries and carried these items back to Babylon (2 Kings 24:13; 25:13-17; 2 Chronicles 36:18; Lamentations 1:10). Others suspect that the Ark was either destroyed with the Temple (2 Chronicles 36:19) or destroyed once it reached Babylon, after being stripped of its gilded outer covering. This theory is reasonable since the destruction of the Temple implied the destruction or plunder of the Temple vessels as well. Nevertheless, this theory faces formidable difficulties.

The first form of the Babylonian theory supposes that the Ark was destroyed either before or with the Temple in 586 B.C. In support of a destruction before that of the Temple, the account in 2 Kings 24:13 says that at the time of Nebuchadnezzar's second invasion, the golden Temple items that Solomon had made were cut in pieces. These gold items are enumerated in 1 Kings 7:48-51 and include an altar, a table of showbread, lampstands, and numerous utensils. Since some of these objects were within the Holy Place, the Ark within the Holy of Holies might have been included.

However, two factors force us to qualify both where and what these vessels must have been. First, the reference to all the vessels of gold which Solomon had made must be qualified by the dual reference in this verse to "all the treasures of the house of the LORD and the treasures of the king's house." As we have seen, this points to the Temple treasuries and not to the inner sanctuary. This qualification is verified by 1 Kings 7:51, which states that the golden utensils were put in "the treasuries of the house of the LORD." These treasuries included duplicates of most of the sacred Temple vessels, including the multiple lampstands. Therefore, there is no need to require these items to have been those in the inner sanctuary. Also, we read of the Babylonian emissary Merodach-baladan being shown the inventory of these very treasuries by King Hezekiah (Isaiah 39:2-6). When the Babylonians next came calling on Jerusalem, they undoubtedly went straight for this treasury, as the prophet had predicted.

Second, at this time, Nebuchadnezzar was only punishing the Jews' insurrection and lack of tribute payment. His soldiers were making collections on Judah's delinquent account. Three deportations (removal of portions of the population) of Jews make up Babylon's response to Judah's "rebellion." This was the second of these, with the destruction of the Temple as a final act of punishment. This being the case, Nebuchadnezzar would not yet have violated the Temple at this stage of his actions. Therefore, the items that Solomon had made and that the Babylonians broke up were only votive gifts deposited in the treasuries of the Temple court.

Even if one could argue that the inner sanctuary was meant, the Ark could not have been included according to the description given, for it was not made by Solomon but by Moses' craftsmen. Also, the biblical lists record that additional Temple vessels were removed 11 years later and transported to Babylon intact. Therefore, these vessels must be different vessels than those captured by Nebuzaradan when he destroyed the Temple. Furthermore, if Nebuzaradan had indeed taken the Ark, he would not have cut it up for bulk gold but would have preserved it intact as a war trophy. It would have been displayed in the Babylonian's temple at Shinar, as were other lesser vessels from the Temple (see Daniel 1:2).

Others have argued that the Ark may have been destroyed in 586 B.C. when Nebuzaradan finally breached the Temple proper and set it on fire. Second Chronicles 36:19 seems to support this when it adds that the invaders "destroyed all its valuable articles." Again, however, we must note that not all of these vessels were destroyed, for according to Daniel 1:2, some of the vessels were deposited in the Babylonian temple. Therefore, on many counts, the Ark could not have been destroyed by the Babylonians.

The biblical account tells us that Nebuchadnezzar plundered the Temple before its destruction and carried off all the articles of the Temple treasuries and "brought them all to Babylon" (2 Kings 24:13; 25:13-17; 2 Chronicles 36:18). Again, the text does not specifically indicate any intrusion into the outer or inner sanctuaries, but the fact that the Temple was burned would probably have required this. Also, the soldiers would probably not have destroyed the Temple without first removing cultic items or objects of value. However, the biblical texts themselves give several reasons why the Ark was not included in this raid.

First, the recorded lists of captured Temple articles never mention the Ark (see 2 Kings 25:13-17; Jeremiah 52:17-23). In fact, they don't mention the capture of *any* of the Temple treasures from the inner sanctuary. Almost every student of the Ark's disappearance has noted this scriptural silence as a significant statement against the Ark's being taken by the Babylonians (or for that matter, by anyone else). Some people have suggested that the reason for this omission was that the Ark had already been destroyed during the second invasion, when the golden vessels were "cut in pieces." However, if the Ark had earlier suffered this fate, it would certainly have been mentioned. The omission of the Ark from any lists of spoils would constitute a great contradiction of biblical history. For example, the account of the Philistine capture of the Ark had warranted *two entire chapters* (1 Samuel 5–6). Surely the Ark could not have been captured or destroyed by the Babylonians without any mention of the fact in such an explicit list. The second-century B.C. historian Eupolemus must have understood this. Writing in agreement with the Jeremiah tradition, he records that the gold and silver vessels of the Temple were seized as tribute and sent to Babylon. But he adds this emphasis: "...except for the Ark and the tablets in it. This Jeremiah preserved" (4.39:5). While 2 Maccabees 2:1-10 includes most all of the treasures being preserved, Eupolemus singles out the Ark as spared the destruction.

Second, all of the vessels taken were later *returned* by the Persians (Ezra 1:7-11). This passage reveals that the Persians had taken an accurate inventory of these items captured from the Babylonians and provided it to the Israelites in Judah for the rebuilding of the Temple. Such a careful accounting in the scriptural texts would certainly have included mention of the most famous object of all—the Ark. Furthermore, these vessels transported by Nebuchadnezzar to

Babylon are apparently the same vessels that Jehoiakim's contemporaries, after his exile, expected to be miraculously returned from Babylon (Jeremiah 27:16–28:6), and still the same ones Cyrus transferred to Sheshbazzar of Judah (Ezra 1:7-11). These vessels, which totaled 5400 (or 5469 according to the Greek version, the Septuagint or LXX), in both name and number do not fit the vessels of the inner sanctuary.

Third, the prophets clearly predicted the Temple vessels would go into captivity, that they would be preserved in Babylon, and that they would be returned *intact* to Jerusalem. Three prophetic texts demonstrate this historical fact. First, Jeremiah 27:16-22 says this: " 'They will be carried to Babylon, and they will be there until the day I visit them,' declares the LORD. 'Then I will bring them back and restore them to this place.' " Next, Daniel 5 reveals that the Temple vessels were unharmed while in Babylon because Belshazzar used them at his great feast. The subsequent events of the chapter show that God continued to watch over these sacred vessels. Once the king employed the Temple vessels in the praise of foreign gods, the hand of Israel's God appeared to declare Babylon's immediate destruction for violating their sanctity, which represented Him, a destruction that occurred that very night. Finally, Isaiah 52:8-12 states that when Judah returned from captivity in Babylon, God would protect the Temple vessels until they reached their destination: "You who carry the vessels of the LORD [back from Babylon]…. the LORD will go before you, and the God of Israel will be your rear guard." These texts confirm that all of the Temple vessels were taken to Babylon, preserved there, and then brought back intact to Jerusalem. Had the Ark been among them, it too would have been restored.

Fourth, one of the purposes for capturing the vessels was to take them to Shinar, where the Babylonian temple was located

(Daniel 1:2). Conquerors often carried off the statues of the gods of those cities they conquered in order to show the superior power of their own gods. This was what the Philistines had done with the Ark hundreds of years earlier (1 Samuel 5:2). The Ark stood for the imageless God of the Jews, so Nebuchadnezzar, who was no doubt familiar with this object from Daniel and the other deportees, would have wanted to secure it for his temple. The fact that he could only deposit the utensils in his temple indicates that he could not obtain the Ark.

However, the apocrypha and the Talmud provide extrabiblical support for this theory in 2 Esdras 10:21-22 and Talmud Babli, *Yoma* 53b. Both of these contend that the Babylonians took the Ark as spoils of battle. The problem with these records is that 2 Esdras was composed at least 600 years after the Babylonian destruction, and the Talmud was not completed for another 200 to 600 years. What this means is that the apocryphal author and the rabbis were attempting to answer an unknown by speculation. As far as we can tell, no historical record or tradition supports this supposition. One Israeli scholar wrote that the Talmudic reference "was based on nothing more than midrashic inferences."[3]

If the Ark was not stolen or destroyed by the Babylonians, it (and the other treasures of the inner sanctuary) must have already been removed prior to this time. In that case, the Ark must have been hidden away. Perhaps the prophetic warnings of God's irrevocable intention to punish Judah by the destruction of the Temple (2 Kings 22:17; 23:26-27) was sufficient cause to remove the Ark to a hiding place to protect it from the threat of enemy discovery and destruction. If this were so, the Levites could have moved it secretly anytime prior to the Babylonian invasion. Fear of subsequent invasions would have kept the Ark in hiding until the right time for its reappearance. This theory of the intentional hiding of the Ark has a long and ancient tradition to support it, and we will explore it together beginning in chapter 9. Before we do, however, let's survey some of the past and present searches for the Ark that have made headlines and continue to appear on our television screens. Come with me as we consider a history of these quests as we move forward in our search for the Ark.

6

Searches for the Ark

Ever since the premiere of the popular movie *Raiders of the Lost Ark,* hardly a year passes without someone claiming to have found the Ark of the Covenant.

—DR. EPHRAIM ISAAC
DIRECTOR, INSTITUTE OF SEMITIC STUDIES, PRINCETON

The Ark of the Covenant has surely been the most sought-after treasure in the history of mankind. Most twenty-first-century people were introduced to the search for the lost Ark on the twentieth-century silver screen, but the quest had been in progress for many centuries before Lawrence Kasdan and George Lucas conceived of Indiana Jones' adventure.

In the nineteenth century, the Western excitement over the new discoveries in the lands of the ancient Near East, and especially the Holy Land, was met by a pressing need to defend the biblical accounts against a tide of modern critics. In those early days of exploration in the Holy Land, archaeology was still in its romance stage. The monumental sculptures and architecture museums acquired from the great empires of Assyria, Babylon, Greece, and Egypt had created an appetite in Western societies. The desire now was for biblical treasures to emerge from Palestine on a scale with the Egyptians pyramids and Grecian temples.

To answer this demand and the challenge of the biblical critics, the Palestine Exploration Fund (PEF) was created. And, interestingly enough, its first publicly supported archaeological expedition was a search for the Ark. Jerusalem author Naomi Shepherd sums up the attitude of the day when she writes, "Evangelical [Christians in Britain] wanted the Ark of the Covenant to be found, as Lord Shaftesbury said, 'as evidence in a day of trouble, of rebuke, and of blasphemy.'" Yet Claude Conder, who went in search of the Ark for the PEF, had to admit upon his return to Great Britain, "We did not bring home the Ark."

Nevertheless a steady stream of Western explorers carried on the search for the Ark as they surveyed, mapped, and identified biblical sites. Some, like the American explorer Antonio Frederick Futterer, chose the area of trans-Jordan (modern Jordan), following the account in 2 Maccabees of the hidden cave under Mount Nebo. But most pursued the Jewish traditions that located the Ark beneath the Temple Mount. Those that did left accounts of torturous descents into wells and subterranean vaults near or on the Temple Mount, often at night in the dead of winter and without lights, with the excited dream of discovering the Ark. While the stories of these men's adventures are legion, one of the most colorful attempts—the Parker Expedition—stands apart from the others in revealing the lengths explorers will go to in their searches for the Ark. We will begin with the account of this early search for the Ark and then move on to more modern searches for the Ark that have brought the Ark to our movie and television screens.

The Parker Expedition

In 1906 Lieutenant Montague Parker, a British officer, resigned from active military duty in England to enlist in a search for the Ark.[1] Unlike his colleagues who had pondered the fate of the Ark while engaged in archaeological surveys in the Holy Land, Parker mounted his expedition with the express purpose of discovering and retrieving the Ark. His lead to its location had come from a Finnish mystic named Valter H. Juvelius, who the same year had delivered a paper at the Swedish University that claimed to provide information showing the hiding place of the Ark under the Temple precincts. The basis for this claim was Juvelius' own discovery of a cryptogram or coded message within the writings of Jeremiah. This message supposedly revealed that Jeremiah had rescued the Ark and hidden it within a secret chamber beneath the Temple Mount. This chamber was, according to Juvelius, accessible through an underground passageway, the place of which, he believed, was also recorded in the cryptogram. Juvelius' paper inspired Parker's decision to leave the service and find the Ark, but Parker's greater motivation was the hope of the notoriety he would gain from such a quest.

After forming a partnership with Juvelius and raising the necessary funding, Parker began searching for the secret passageway, guided by a Danish clairvoyant hired by Juvelius. His search began by tracing Charles Warren's investigation of the area of the Gihon Spring (the Virgin's Fountain, so-called because tradition taught that the Virgin Mary drew water from it). This spring was the northern entrance to Hezekiah's Water Tunnel, a 1750-foot-long subterranean conduit commissioned by the Judean king Hezekiah in 701 B.C. Juvelius believed that it might connect with the secret chamber where the Ark was hidden, and so under the guise of acquiring property to build schools and hospitals for the people on behalf of the Turkish government, they took control of a site on the southern slope of the City of David and began clearing one of Warren's shafts in hopes of finding access to the chamber. However, lack of archaeological knowledge, severe winter rains, and an excess of dinner parties[2] soon exhausted Parker's funds and forced him to return home to get more money and a fresh team.

Upon returning to Jerusalem, Parker soon discovered that his formerly favorable circumstances had changed and that his project now faced opposition from both the Turks and the Jews. The Jews, through the aid of financier Edmond de Rothschild, had purchased a plot of ground nearby Parker's and had begun competitive excavations. The Turks ordered Parker to finish his work within the year. Faced with this hopeless situation, the pressure from expectant donors, and a winter of work without results, Parker resorted to desperate measures.

Bypassing his plan to tunnel to the *haram,* the sacred Muslim enclosure on Mount Moriah on which stood the Al-Aqsa Mosque and the Dome of the Rock, and under which Parker believed the chamber of the Ark to be located, he set upon digging directly on the site. His new plan was to bribe the Turkish pasha of Jerusalem, Amzey Bey, and the guardian of the Dome of the Rock, Sheikh Khalil, to allow him and his team (disguised as Arabs) to secretly dig within the *haram*. However, after a week of work, and coming no closer to a tunnel, Parker turned his attention to the "Well of the Souls," a subterranean drain located below the cave floor of the great stone in the Dome of the Rock. Understanding that for a foreigner to be caught outside on the *haram* meant instant death, Parker perhaps figured he could do no worse inside the Muslim shrine. Parker and his team entered the Dome of the Rock and worked under cover of night for a week, with Parker breaking up the huge flagstones within the shrine to get to the anticipated passageway. But early on the morning of the eighth day, a Muslim cleric saw some of Parker's workers in the shadows dumping baskets of rubble. Not knowing of Parker's deal with the government authorities, the cleric sounded the alarm. As word spread throughout the populace, the city became riotous. Muslims rushed toward the sacred site to avenge its desecration as Parker and his team fled for their lives to their yacht anchored at the port of Jaffa and immediately set sail.

The Search for the Ark Continues

Claude Conder's sad statement, "We did not bring home the Ark," did not discourage others in this quest. In fact, it made them all the more determined. The international success of *The Raiders of the Lost Ark* created a new market for Ark research. With the advent of 24-hour programming and the proliferation of adventure and history channels, the demand for shows on archaeological treasures, and particularly documentaries on the Ark of the Covenant, has increased. Since Indiana Jones lost the Ark to a government warehouse, searches for the Ark have been proposed or conducted at the Dead Sea, Ein-Gedi, the Mount of Olives, Mount Nebo, Gordon's Calvary, Abu Gosh (Kiriath-jearim), the West Bank village of Dhahiriya, Egypt, Ethiopia, a Knights Templar cathedral in France, and a castle in Ireland! Several of these searches have captured worldwide attention through regularly aired documentaries, including the Ethiopian theory, the Egyptian–West Bank theory, and the Knights Templar theory. We will first survey some of these theories, reserving the more popular Ethiopian theory for the next chapter.

Is the Ark in the West Bank?

A national television documentary proposed that the Ark rests within a wall in the politically contested territory of the West Bank. This claim is made by Michael Sanders, the British-born publisher of classical university texts, who now lives in Irvine, California. Believing the Ark was taken by the Egyptian pharaoh Shishak when he invaded the First Temple complex at the beginning of his raids on Jerusalem (about 925 B.C.), Sanders imagined that the Ark might still be buried in the place where Shishak took it. Using information concerning Shishak's invasion contained in the Harris Papyrus, an Egyptian document in the British Museum, he started searching for a geographic clue to where the army took its captured loot. Knowing that Egyptian practice was to house plundered artifacts, especially religious documents, within their temples, Sanders reasoned:

> This temple is referred to in the papyrus as a 'mysterious house in the land of Zahi' which was dedicated to the god Amun Ra.... If the Egyptians had just seized the most sacred religious codes from the people they had invaded, they would have laid them in the foundations of their new temple.[3]

He then concluded that the broken stone tablets of the Ten Commandments, which once resided within the Ark, would have been buried in this Egyptian temple in a post-battle ritual. For Sanders, the Ark was not as important as the broken pieces of the Israelite law code. He says,

> If there is any power or mystique associated with the Ark, it does not rest with the box, it rests in the stones. Did Steven Spielberg in *Raiders of the Lost Ark* stumble on the truth when he shows that when the Ark was opened, what appeared was not a set of stones but a great energy and power?[4]

The next task for Sanders was to discover the present-day location of this Egyptian temple. In his research he found that in 1830 the American explorer Edward Robinson claimed to have walked Shishak's invasion route in Israel and found old ruins at an Arab village called Dhahiriya. Today this village, located at the southern edge of the West Bank near Hebron, is under control of the Palestinian Authority and is a notorious training ground for Hamas terrorists. Satellite images of the region led Sanders to identify the modern site of the Egyptian temple with a ruin south of the settlement. In a program aired on ABC television, Sanders presented his evidence and then led a film crew to the site of "the ruins," a wall in a trash-laden area of the Palestinian town. With wide-eyed Palestinian children watching, he pointed to a section at the corner of the wall, behind which he contended the stone tablets of the Ark could still lie buried. In spite of his knowledge that the village was under the control of a local sheikh, and that he had no prior contact with him or with the Palestinian authorities, he went on camera into the city office and asked for permission to excavate at the site of the wall. He was, of course, refused; an action that he bitterly protested (again on camera) as though a great injustice had been done. The program concluded with the prospect that the treasure of the Ark might still remain hidden behind the wall!

Sanders has concluded other explorations in much the same manner. Before his search for the Ark, he searched for the site of Sodom and Gomorrah beneath the northern end of the Dead Sea with a yellow submarine. Believing that satellite photos of the area revealed traces of ancient structures beneath the waters, he launched his search for the famed cities with the yellow submarine in a much publicized (and televised) manner. In the end all he discovered were ridges in the salt formations of the Dead

Sea floor, which however, he continued to offer as possibly the remains of walls. The problem with the "evidence" that Sanders uses to connect his various deductions is that his evidence is itself his personal deduction. It is a deduction that Shishak captured Temple treasures and an even greater deduction that the Ark was among them. As I have explained in chapter 3, the biblical text does not imply that Shishak invaded the Temple and took its treasures. Instead, it clearly states that the golden shields in the royal storehouses were plundered. Given such a specific reference to an object that was captured, it is simply impossible that the seizure of the greatest object of Israel's worship could take place without even a historical footnote! Furthermore, Sanders, like all who adopt the Shishak theory, fails to deal adequately with the distinct mention of the Ark at the time of King Josiah (620 B.C.) more than 400 years later (see 2 Chronicles 35:3). If the Ark was not taken by Shishak, then all of Sanders' elaborate theory is unfounded. There is also no warrant for the deduction that Shishak took any loot plundered from the Jerusalem raids to an Egyptian temple. Most scholars, as previously noted, believe that any gold from Solomon's storehouses ended up in Tanis within the *tomb* of Shishak. Edward Robinson may have traced the route of Shishak through Dhahiriya, but he did not suggest that an Egyptian temple was there. Moreover, there is no reason to deduce that a wall in a Palestinian village is the remains of an Egyptian temple unless one presents comparative evidence from actual Egyptian temples. Finally, to believe that a permit from the authorities to excavate could be received on demand is both unprofessional and impudent. Sanders' theory certainly makes for great entertainment, but without historical accuracy or supporting evidence required by the archaeological method, it is really nothing more than entertainment.

The Search in a Knights Templar Cathedral

The Crusaders, who were mostly French, were quite successful in their first attempts to take the Holy Land from the Muslims in 1099. They even succeeded in capturing and holding the city of Jerusalem and establishing a French-born king (who claimed to be a descendant of David) over the city. Shortly after that, an order of knights known as the Knights Templar was formed in Jerusalem. The purpose of the Knights Templar was to protect Jerusalem and to aid European pilgrims coming to the Holy Land. Over the next hundred years, this small group of knights not only grew in number, but they also grew unbelievably in wealth. In fact, these men became the first international bankers, loaning money to kings and nobles throughout Europe. How they acquired their immense wealth has been the subject of great speculation. The headquarters for the Knights Templar was in the Mosque of Omar, that is, the Dome of the Rock, which sits on the site of the old Temple. Some people have suggested that the knights excavated the tunnels beneath the mosque and found the treasures of Solomon's Temple, and that was the source of their wealth.

But then the king of France decided he no longer wanted the knights around. He accused their members of hideous sins and atrocities. They were arrested and tortured to force them to confess to his trumped-up charges. Those who confessed were locked away in prisons; those who refused were tortured to death or burned at the stake. Two of the last to be executed in this way were Jacques de Molay, the Grand Master of the Knights Templar, and Geoffrey de Charney, Preceptor of Normandy. (Geoffrey de Charney apparently was the uncle of the later Geoffrey de Charney, who was the first person that we can positively determine had possession of the Shroud of Turin.)

According to this theory, the Knights Templar may have taken the Ark and the other Temple treasures from Israel and hidden them in southern France. If so, it is conjectured, many of the treasures and the Ark may still be there, hidden away. In fact, a secret society in France called the Prieure de Sion traces its origins to the Knights Templar. According to authors Baigent, Leigh, and Lincoln, the head of the society was quoted as saying that he knows where the Temple treasures are and that they will be returned to Jerusalem "when the time is right."

Many books make diverse claims about the Knights Templar. History has concluded generally that this secret society was heretical and bent on obtaining political and religious power. Despite their control of the Dome of the Rock and the rumor of clandestine searches beneath the site, no record of their finding the Ark has surfaced. Due to the nature of their bizarre activities and the unfounded claims attributed to them by recent sensationalist authors, it is best to ignore such accounts as fanciful fictions.

In surveying some of these recent searches for the Ark, we have yet to explore one of the most popular theories for its location—the country of Ethiopia. We now want to join that expedition in the next chapter.

7
Is the Ark in Ethiopia?

In Ethiopia today one can hardly find a single individual out of a population of sixty million who harbors the slightest doubt that the ark lies quietly in state in the chapel at Axum.[1]

—Robert Cornuke and David Halbrook

One of the most widely advanced theories for the location of the Ark is that it resides in Ethiopia. According to proponents of this view, the Ark was removed from the Jerusalem Temple either during the reign of Solomon (970–930 B.C.) in the invasion of Shishak (926 B.C.), or during the time of Manasseh (687–642 B.C.). It either went directly to Axum, Ethiopia, or resided for a time in the Jewish temple on Elephantine Island before being housed in Axum. Today it still exists within the Chapel of the Tablet in the Abyssinian Church of Saint Mary of Zion under the careful watch of a guardian, appointed for life to preserve its sanctity and protect it from outsiders.

The Ethiopian Legend of the Ark

The belief that the Ark is in Ethiopia is based on a national epic known as the Ethiopian Royal Chronicles and called the *Kebra Negast* ("Glory of the Kings"). The official version was translated into Ge'ez between 1314 and 1344 by Yeshaq of Axum, although its origins may come from several centuries before.[2] "Its purpose," according to Edwin Yamauchi, "was to lend support to the new 'Solomonic' dynasty that had gained power in 1270, replacing the Zagwe dynasty."[3] The head of this dynasty, Yekuno Amlak, who ruled from A.D. 1274 to 1285, secured his royal ascendancy based on his claim to be the descendant of Solomon and the queen of Sheba. The *Kebra Negast* was composed to document the history behind this claim.

The *Kebra Negast* tells of the story of the visit of the queen of Sheba to King Solomon in Jerusalem. While there she conceived a child by Solomon. She returned home to bear a son, whom she named Menelik ("son of the king"). After Menelik had grown up, he journeyed to Jerusalem to learn from his father and decided to steal the Ark of the Covenant. Solomon and his army pursued him as far as Egypt but finally gave up, and Menelik returned to Ethiopia with the Ark. Another version of the story says that a Jewish priest named Azarias substituted imitation tablets for the real Mosaic Tablets and spirited the originals away, later revealing them to Menelik, to his great delight. Yet another version contends that the entire Ark was replaced with a copy, and the genuine article was taken to Ethiopia with Menelik's party. Some versions justify Menelik's hasty departure, looting of the Temple, and deception, by stating that the Ethiopian party left Jerusalem because of the jealousy of the priests, and they took the Ark in order to protect it from idolatry (such as that of Manasseh, who would later defile the Temple). Thus, they carried the Ark to safety in Ethiopia.

Each year in late November, the date Menelik is said to have brought the Ark to Axum, a celebration takes place in the city. According to the *Kebra Negast,* this follows a precedent set by the queen of Sheba, who invited the public to a feast in honor of her son's return. At this annual ceremony called the *Timkat*, the *tabot* (one of many replicas of the Ark) is removed from the Axum church and paraded through the street, symbolizing the traditional journey of the Ark from Jerusalem to the sacred city.

An Ethiopian priest balances on his head a chest containing a replica of the Ark during the Timkat ceremony. Photo courtesy of Chuck Missler.

Ethiopian Theory Proponents

In the early 1990s, British journalist Graham Hancock brought the Ethiopian tradition to the attention of the West with his book *The Sign and the Seal: The Quest for the Lost Ark of the Covenant* and subsequent television documentaries. Another British team of authors, Roderick Grierson and Stuart Munro-Hay, adopted the same theory in their book *The Ark of the Covenant*, but they were much more critical in their dealing with the ancient sources. Canadian author Grant Jeffrey's *Unveiling Mysteries of the Bible* and Bob Cornuke and David Halbrook's *In Search of the Lost Ark of the Covenant* have also adopted this theory and have added their respective contributions of personal interview and exploration.

Hancock traced the legend of the Ark through modern times and traditions, connecting it with the Knights Templar and their search for the Holy Grail, as well as other traditions. His views include interpreting Moses as an Egyptian magician and rejecting the historicity of the biblical text. His historical interpretations are often forced in his attempt to trace the route of the Ark to Ethiopia. For example, Hancock rejects the *Kebra Negast* account and argues that the Ark must have been brought to Elephantine Island because the Jews in exile built a temple there but not in Babylon, where the rest of the Jewish population had been deported. The explanation for this, however, has nothing to do with the Ark. The Jewish exiles in Egypt had fled there to seek refuge from the Babylonian invaders, whereas those Jews in Babylon were captives. The Jewish settlement at Elephantine had freedom of worship due to its geographical distance from Babylon, whereas in Babylon the exiles were subject to the Babylonian political and religious system. Moreover, the temple at Elephantine could not have been constructed to house the Ark because the Torah forbade construction of a temple anywhere but Jerusalem. Even though the Jerusalem Temple had been destroyed, a foreign temple, though Jewish, was still illegitimate, and to install the Ark there would have been an unorthodox act.[4]

Grierson and Munro-Hay analyze the Ethiopian accounts in an attempt to trace the origins of the object deposited in the Axum church. Their research shows how Abyssinian Christianity absorbed Jewish customs and in doing so may have reinterpreted the Israelite Ark in Christian terms. Following this line of reasoning, they draw their conclusions as to what the object in the church might be. However, in the end, they prefer a mystical rather than literal meaning for the secret of the "Ark at Axum." By contrast, Jeffrey, Cornuke, and Halbrook uncritically accept Ethiopian claims of the Ark at Axum, trading scholarship for a detective search as they relate personal encounters and interviews with government and religious clerics who maintain the official position. Such an approach leads Jeffrey to believe the Ark was moved from Axum to outside Jerusalem in 1991, while Cornuke and Halbrook's sources insist it never left Axum.

Cornuke and Halbrook also advance a unique view, based on their interpretation of certain prophetic texts in the Bible, that the Ethiopian government will return the Ark when Christ returns so that it can serve as His throne in the Millennial Temple. They likewise explain that the mission behind the Ethiopian eunuch's visit to Jerusalem (Acts 8:26-40) was to check out the rumors that the Messiah had come in order to return the Ark (which was part of Queen Candace's treasure, Acts 8:27) as a gift in harmony with the prophecy of Zephaniah 3:10. Accepting these views, evangelical author and teacher Chuck Missler has suggested an additional piece to the historical puzzle. He believes that pharaoh Shishak took the Ark of the Covenant to Egypt shortly after the death of Solomon. Consequently, it came into Ethiopian possession when Ethiopia took over Egypt and ruled it during the twenty-fifth (Ethiopian) dynasty. He has explained King Josiah's attack on the Egyptian pharaoh Neco II (whom he says was the last of the Ethiopian dynasty) at Megiddo as an attempt to return the Ark to Israel, since the pharaoh was carrying it with him to confront the Chaldeans at Carchemish (2 Chronicles 35:20-27). I will interact with these ideas in more detail in chapter 11.

Problems with the Ethiopian Theory

The first problem with this theory is that it is based on the fourteenth-century A.D. Ethiopian Royal Chronicles, the *Kebra Negast.* Every historical reconstruction of the route of the Ark to Ethiopia and interviews with alleged eyewitnesses of the Ark in Axum are influenced by this document. Although the *Kebra Negast* is the national epic of Ethiopia and is held to be historical fact by both government officials and clerics of the Ethiopian Orthodox Church, it is judged by historians as a legendary account created for propagandistic purposes.

Its character as legend can be seen from its many mythological elements. For example, it describes the Ark as having its own will, deciding to leave Jerusalem on its own. It depicts the Ark as moving by its own magical power to Africa, empowering the men, animals, and equipment in Menelik's party to make the trip to Egypt in a single day by flying. The *Kebra Negast* attributes magical powers to King Solomon, as well as the ability to talk with birds and animals and to create a flying vessel as a gift for the queen of Sheba. It claims that Menelik took the Ark "in the twinkling of an eye" with the help of the Angel of the Lord, and the archangel Michael flew over Menelik's party and parted the sea so they could march on dry ground. The legend states that the Ark destroyed all of Egypt's idols as it flew overhead with the Ethiopians, and that without the Ark to magically supply Solomon's wisdom, he became foolish and idolatrous. Menelik supposedly took the Ark to war and defeated (by the Ark's power) a city of vipers with the faces of men and the tails of asses attached to their bellies. Even the description of the queen of Sheba as an Ethiopian is mythical. Historians agree that she was not from Ethiopia but was from Saba in southern Arabia (modern Yemen) and ruled over the Sabeans. Ethiopia was not involved in the politics of the day because in the tenth century B.C. (the time of Solomon), Ethiopian (Nubian) settlements were too small to support an empire. The queen of Sheba most likely made her visit to Solomon because of the concern that his presence in the Gulf of Aqaba threatened the caravan routes upon which southern Arabia depended.

A second problem of the Ethiopian theory is the late date of its origin. Dr. Steven Kaplan, Chairman of the Hebrew University's African Studies Department, claims in his book *The Beta Israel in Ethiopia: From Earliest Times to the Twentieth Century* that Ethiopian Jewry can only be traced back 600 years to some time between the fourteenth and sixteenth centuries.[5] The facts above argue against a date of composition earlier than the fourteenth century A.D., more than 2000 years after the events it describes! The Ethiopian national epic declares that Ethiopian rulers are descended from Solomon and that the Ark is in Ethiopia. The reasons for this assertion can be traced to a political and religious conflict in the nation's history.

The *Kebra Negast* reveals that it was composed when Judaism and Christianity were in conflict in the region. A conflict also arose between two kings who claimed to maintain the succession from Solomon, which was essential for the royal house to maintain its position. Harry Atkins, who researched Ethiopian history as a lecturer for the Ethiopian government at the Menelik II School in Addis Ababa, contends that there was no record of the Ark being in Ethiopia until the end of the thirteenth century. He offers this explanation: "At that time there was a dispute over who should be king. One of the claimants to the throne said he was a descendant of King Solomon and the Queen of Sheba. When Ykuna Amlak became king (1274–1285 A.D.), the legend of the Ark being in Ethiopia entered Ethiopian history."[6]

A further problem is that the Solomonic emperors of Ethiopia believed that Ethiopia was the new Israel and that Jews were a threat. For this reason replacement theology, the view that Christianity replaced Israel as God's chosen people, is the perspective in the *Kebra Negast.* The Ark, we are told, was from the beginning of its creation "Christian," being made by the Holy Trinity. The Ark prefigures the womb of the Virgin Mary, for God lived in it just as He later would in the mother of the Redeemer. Solomon receives a dream that shows Israel rejecting the glory of God, and the glory moves to the Ethiopian Christian community forever—or at least until Christ returns, at which time the Ark would return to Him. At that time it will be opened and the heavenly objects inside will condemn the Jews. Because Ethiopia and not Israel possesses the Ark, they alone have the blessing of God. This viewpoint supports a medieval date of the legend's origin and points to a political and religious rivalry as its cause.

Of course, the theory has logical problems, foremost of which is how the Ark could have been secreted out of the Holy of Holies and removed from Jerusalem. Rabbi Goren contended that no one—not even the legitimate Zadokite priests—could possibly have had unguarded access to the Ark: "Nobody could make switches, and nobody had free access to the Ark. Whatever time [of day or night] it was—even on Yom Kippur when [the high priest] had just a few minutes inside—they wouldn't let anyone go inside. They would kill them!"[7]

To appreciate just how impossible it would have been for a priest to snatch the Ark, consider the ancient record of how carefully the entrance to the Temple was guarded:

> As the "family" whose daily "ministration was accomplished" left the Temple, the massive gates were closed by priests or Levites, some requiring the united

strength of twenty men. Then the Temple keys were hung up...[in] the chief guardroom of the priests.... Already the night watches had been set in the Temple. By day and night it was the duty of the Levites to guard the gates, to prevent, so far as possible; the unclean from entering.... At night guards were placed in twenty-four stations about the gates and courts. Of these twenty-one were occupied by Levites alone; the other innermost three jointly by priests and Levites. Each guard consisted of ten men; so that in all two hundred and forty Levites and thirty priests were on duty every night. The Temple guards were relieved by day, but not during the night, which the Romans divided into four, but the Jews, properly, into three watches, the fourth being really the morning watch.... During the night the "captain of the Temple" made his rounds. On his approach the guards had to rise and salute him in a particular manner. Any guard found asleep when on duty was beaten, or his garments were set on fire—a punishment, as we know, actually awarded.... But, there could have been little inclination to sleep within the Temple, even had the deep emotions natural in the circumstances allowed it... [for] the preparations for the service of the morning required each to be early astir. The priest whose duty it was to superintend might any moment knock at the door and unexpectedly, no one knew when.... Those who were prepared now followed the superintending priest.... One company passed eastwards, the other westwards, till, having made their circuit of inspection, they met at the chamber where the high priest's daily

> meat-offering was prepared, and reported, "It is well! All is well!"[8]

A final and, according to my interpretation, insurmountable problem is the biblical statement of the chronicler (2 Chronicles 35:3) that the Ark was still in the Temple in the time of King Josiah (622 B.C.). Hancock (followed by Missler) believes that this passage teaches the opposite, namely, that the Ark was *not* still in the Temple at this time. His only argument for this is that the Levites did not appear to obey Josiah's request to bring back the Ark to the Temple. He notes that the Bible records no installation service. He also connects 2 Chronicles 35:3 with Jeremiah 3:16, which he believes announces the disappearance of the Ark. Therefore, he contends that the Levites could not obey Josiah's request because the Ark had already been taken to Ethiopia. But there is no warrant for assuming that the Levites did not obey Josiah's command. If the Ark was gone, a fact that the Levites would have known, how could the king have issued the order? Furthermore, the chronicler is describing Josiah's religious successes and Temple reform. It seems incredible that he would have preserved an embarrassing account of Israel's failure to restore the most significant item of Temple worship. This is consistent with the chronicler's pattern of promoting a positive image of the Temple and the Ark. Jeremiah's statement, as many commentators agree, does not imply that the Ark was no longer in existence when Jeremiah wrote this verse toward the end of the monarchy. Rather, it may be a text that offers the hope of the Ark's preservation and future restoration in Judah.

What *Is* in Ethiopia?

Despite the late date and legendary nature of the Ethiopian story, the Ethiopian church as well as government officials believe they are in possession of an object they believe to be the Ark. Authors Cornuke and Halbrook state that "from the lowliest peasant to the highest public official, all insist that, secured within the shadows of St. Mary of Zion's fortified inner sanctum, separated from the outside world only by a high fence and a lonely guardian, sits a wooden chest of biblical significance."[9] According to Cornuke and Halbrook, it is even registered annually in a government inventory of national treasures stored in the Axum repository. *World Net Daily* writer Kaye Corbett has observed, "It's so integrated into the nation's psyche that there's a replica of it in more than 20,000 Ethiopian Orthodox churches throughout the world. It is their source of strength, their reason for living."[10] If the Ethiopians have such a consensus of belief—and indeed something is in the Chapel of the Tablet—we must ask, What is this object?

The Ethiopian scholar Ephraim Isaac investigated this question and observed, "All Christians have some form of an altar." He supposed the Ethiopian ark might be such an ancient altar. "Even if the Ark is some sort of an ancient Semitic ritual object," he queried, "is what the Ethiopians possess the original Israelite object?" No definitive answer can be given to this question because no image of the object has ever been published. The historical descriptions given by eyewitnesses are all that we have to go on.

The earliest known depiction comes from the thirteenth-century Armenian writer Abu Salih, who claimed to have seen the Ark in use in an Ethiopian Christian mass:

> The Abyssinians possess also the Ark of the Covenant, in which are the two tablets of stone, inscribed by the finger of God with the commandments which he ordained for the children of Israel. The Ark of the

> Covenant is placed upon the altar, but it is not so wide as the altar; it is as high as the knee of a man, and is overlaid with gold; and upon its upper cover there are crosses of gold; and there are five precious stones upon it, one at each of the four corners, and one in the middle."[11]

Grierson and Munro-Hay believe this refers only to a lid that covered the Ark or that the object was not that in the Church of Mary Zion in Axum but in another church, possibly the church of Beta Maryam at Lalibela.[12] However, we have no reason to believe Abu Salih was in any other than the place where he was told the Solomonic Ark was enshrined. We must note two critical observations concerning this account, however. First, Abu Salih did not see the two tablets but only related the belief that they were there. Second, despite the resemblances to the Old Testament Ark, the differences are far more striking. Abu Salih doesn't mention the mercy seat and the cherubim, and the gold box is adorned with crosses and jewels. Nevertheless, as Grierson and Munro-Hay acknowledge, Abu Salih still believed he was in the presence of the biblical relic and that it contained the Mosaic tablets. So even though this depiction reveals an obviously Christian relic, it was still accepted as the Israelite Ark.

Most historical accounts of the object in Axum refer to it as a stone or tablet. In 1520 the European chaplain Francisco Alvares described the object as an ancient stone altar brought from Jerusalem. From the same time (1534) comes the statement of the senior Ethiopian cleric Saga Za-Ab in relating a version of the *Kebra Negast* legend that only the Mosaic tablets had been taken from the Ark in Jerusalem and brought to Ethiopia. Another story, composed in this same period, is taken from the Islamic record known as "The Conquest of Abyssinia." It tells of the emperor Lebna Dengel, who conquered the city of Axum and ordered "the great idol" to be removed from the church of Axum. The "idol" was described as a white stone encrusted with gold that was so large it would not fit through the doors and so heavy 400 men were needed to transport it. According to the story it was deposited in a fortress in the country of Shire.

Modern eyewitness accounts seem to agree with these old portrayals of the Ark as a stone object. According to author Nicholas Clapp, the select priests and monks who have been allowed into the Chapel of the Tablet for ritual purposes "have described the Ark as a single polished stone tablet on which the Ten Commandments are inscribed in Hebrew. The tablet is two and a half feet long and one and a half inches thick; it rests in an unadorned hinged box, three inches thick, of solid hammered gold. Similarly, Fantahune Melaku, an Ethiopian immigrant to Israel I interviewed in Israel, said that "once a man named Ademas received permission and was allowed even to enter into the cement vaults below the church, if he promised not to talk about what he saw. What he said that he saw were *titles* written in Hebrew letters."[13] I was working through a translator when I received this statement, so I asked for clarification of the translation "titles." Melaku said that he saw a stone like a pillar that was inscribed with writing he believed was Hebrew. This account accords with the early descriptions of a stone tablet being identified as the Ark.

In light of this discussion, it is significant that *tabot,* the Ethiopian term for the Ark, is used for wooden tablets written or engraved on wood and housed within a chest. Examples were captured from Ethiopia during the Napier expedition to Abyssinia (1867–1868) and are presently housed in the Ethnographic Store in Hackney, England, as part of the Holmes collection. Pictures of these *tabotat* show square and rectangular wooden slabs approximately 18 inches long and wide, and about 3 inches thick. The writing on these slabs is in Ge'ez, the liturgical language, and they are inscribed with crosses and other ornamentation. Such *tabotat* (replicas of the Ark) must exist in every Orthodox church in the country, and worshippers drape them in brocade and carry them in chests on their heads in the annual *Timkat* procession. However, the word *tabot* can refer equally to a stone altar tablet, an inscribed wooden slab, and even the chest in which the tablet is kept, so it is unclear whether their close association permitted the same word to be used for each or if this usage reflects a medieval confusion with a Christian artifact as the *Kebra Negast* legend became a part of Abyssinian Christianity. Grierson and Munro-Hay comment concerning the possibility of such confusion:

> Could it have been an altar stone of great antiquity that began to be called the Ark of the Covenant at a later date, when Ethiopian Christians became increasingly fascinated with the Old Testament, or when they came under pressure from Jesuit missionaries to explain the number of Old Testament customs that they preserved? Although the Tabernacle and the Temple were provided with objects that were specifically called altars and were distinct from the Ark, it is certainly true that on the Day of Atonement the cover of the Ark was sprinkled with blood in the manner we might expect of an altar. And given that the sacrifice of Christ, according to the account of the Tabernacle in the Epistle to the Hebrews, replaced the ritual of the Day of Atonement, it would be quite reasonable for the Tablet of Moses and the altar stone to be identified. If the great relic were an altar stone, could it still

> be an Ark? The answer may seem to defy logic, but it would nevertheless appear that it could.[14]

Grierson and Munro-Hay relate numerous old accounts, some from actual guardians of the Axum shrine, that the Chapel of the Tablet in fact contained only the tablet of Moses. They contend that even though this conflicts with the twelfth-century *Kebra Negast* legend, the evidence from earlier centuries made the same claim but has been largely ignored.[15] Also, the Ethiopians have preserved many ancient Israelite customs. If they actually possessed the Ark of the Covenant, we must wonder why they would not have built a temple to house it in accord with the Old Testament precedent (2 Chronicles 5:7). While this may again reflect confusion, equating a Christian church with a Jewish temple, it could also imply an original understanding that they possessed only an altar stone (which they equated with the tablet of Moses and later with the Ark itself), so no temple was required.

Whatever is within the Axum church, millions of Ethiopians who have never seen the actual object have enshrined the belief that it is the Ark.

In chapter 11 we will again consider the question of what is within the Axum shrine, hearing what two very contradictory eyewitnesses say they saw within the Chapel of the Tablet. But first we will turn to a different historical tradition concerning the hidden Ark that bears even closer scrutiny.

PART 3

Searching the Temple Mount for the Ark

8
The Hidden Ark

For nothing is hidden, except to be revealed;
nor has anything been secret,
but that it would come to light.

—MARK 4:22

The Ark of the Covenant has always been shrouded in mystery. From the beginning, it was hidden from public view and approachable by only a select few. When the Israelites transported it, they had to keep it covered throughout its journey (Numbers 4:5-6). Once the Levites placed it within the Holy of Holies, they hung a specially constructed curtain to prevent direct access to the Ark. No one, not even a priest, could enter "beyond the veil"—an expression still used today of forbidden territory. Once the priests installed the Ark within the Temple, the high priest alone was allowed to enter the presence of the Ark, and that for only a few minutes once a year (on the Day of Atonement). Even then, he did not actually see the Ark. The Holy of Holies was an unlighted, windowless room. One of the names for the Holy of Holies is the Inner Sanctum, a term for that which is terrifying and mysterious. And the concealment of the Ark did not stop there. To make absolutely certain the high priest did not inadvertently look upon the Ark, he was commanded by law to carry burning incense, which produced thick smoke that had to completely fill the room before he could approach the mercy seat of the Ark.

To add to the high anxiety that the nation of Israel felt on this occasion, the high priest had to wear bells on his robe so that people could hear that he was still alive once inside the Holy of Holies. Moreover, the Zohar (a text of Hasidic Judaism) records the tradition that people outside the Holy Place took precautions for removing the high priest's body (by means of a rope attached to his ankle) if he should have an improper thought while performing his duties before the Ark and be killed.[1] Just as mountain climbers tie themselves together when they are in treacherous terrain, the high priest was attached by a rope to priests outside. If the unexpected happened, they could withdraw his corpse from within the sacred place without risking certain death to retrieve it.

These examples explain why the Ark was concealed from human contact and hidden from public view. If the Ark was hidden from the gaze of God's chosen people, the theory that the Ark was hidden from the desecration of pagan invaders should come as no surprise.

In this chapter we will begin to examine the theory that the Ark was hidden in antiquity with the intention of later returning it to its place in the Temple. We will start by considering the precedent recorded in the Old Testament for hiding sacred objects, especially within the Temple. We will then survey the rich traditions of the hiding of the Temple treasures, and finally we will consider some of the hiding places for the Ark researchers suggest.

Hiding the Book of the Covenant

The Old Testament suggests that the original autograph of the book of the covenant had been hidden somewhere in the

Temple by faithful priests to prevent it from being destroyed during the idolatrous reigns of Manasseh or Amon. It was discovered in the time of Josiah when repairs were made to the sanctuary (2 Chronicles 34:14-30). The Jewish writer Ben Sira (190–180 B.C.) believed the book of the covenant included the entire five books of the Torah given to Moses (Sirach 24:23). We know that the original Torah was kept alongside the Ark in the Temple (Deuteronomy 31:24-26). If the Torah was hidden to protect it from threat, the Ark, beside which it was deposited, would also be likely to have been hidden. Though the Bible does not tell us what happened to the Ark, Jewish scholars drew implications from the text of 2 Chronicles 35 and developed detailed traditions concerning the hiding place of the Ark and other Temple treasures.

The Ark as Part of the Treasures of the Temple

The Temple treasure consists of the original vessels constructed by Moses' craftsmen in the Sinai Desert. These included the furniture in the Tabernacle, which was later transferred with the dismantled Tabernacle to the First Temple by Solomon. We read about this in 1 Kings 8:4 (see 2 Chronicles 5:5): "They brought up the ark of the LORD and the tent of meeting and all the holy utensils, which were in the tent, and the priests and the Levites brought them up."

Note that these vessels were kept with the Mosaic tent. Solomon had made new vessels for the Temple because it was greatly expanded and more lavishly adorned than the Tabernacle (1 Kings 7:48-50; 2 Chronicles 4:19-22). According to various Jewish traditions, the treasured items from the Tabernacle were kept with the Tabernacle itself. These included the Ark of the Covenant (Exodus 25:10-22) and the objects kept with it (the tablets of the law, the original Torah, the golden pot of manna, the rod of Aaron that budded, the golden tumors of the Philistines, and a jar of anointing oil). We are not told where Solomon placed the golden table of showbread (Exodus 25:23-30), the golden lampstand (Exodus 25:31-40), and the golden altar of incense (Exodus 30:1-10), but the Ark of the Covenant was placed in the Holy of Holies between two newly constructed olivewood cherubim. The other items may have been put in their original settings as in the Tabernacle or stored with it somewhere within the confines of the Temple itself (see chapter 11). These vessels had a unique sanctity because they alone had been made by God's direct order and design (Exodus 25:8-9,40), and they connected Israel with Moses and the nation's constitutional foundation.

None of these treasures of the Temple were included among the some 5400 gold, silver, and bronze vessels captured by the Babylonians during their three pillages of the First Temple in 605 B.C., 597 B.C., and 586 B.C. They are not included in the lists of items returned by Sheshbazzar of Judah (2 Kings 24:13; 25:14-15; 2 Chronicles 36:18; Ezra 1:8-11; Daniel 1:2). The Jews therefore presumed that the Babylonians either destroyed these original vessels (see 2 Kings 25:13; Jeremiah 3:16) or that the Jews hid them away before the Babylonian invasion to preserve them for a later time of restoration (see 2 Chronicles 35:3; Ezekiel 43:4-5; 44:27; Haggai 2:8-9).

What the Ancient Sources Say

Jewish traditions outside the Bible sought to explain what had happened to the Tabernacle, the Ark of the Covenant, the great menorah, the altar of incense, and all the most important vessels and treasures of the First and Second Temples. Without these items, the Jews could not envision the complete restoration to "greater glory" than that of First Temple times that the prophets predicted (see Haggai 2:7-9). Therefore, these traditions use prophetic figures such as Jeremiah or his scribe Baruch as spokesmen. Jeremiah had prophesied the destruction of the First Temple, so these texts make him responsible for overseeing the preservation of its sacred vessels. In addition, he had made predictions concerning the final restoration of Israel's glory, and all of these accounts appear to focus on these last days.[2] Our purpose here is not to evaluate the accuracy of these sources but to study them for what they reveal concerning the tradition of the Temple treasure.

Jeremiah Hides the Temple Vessels

The author of the apocryphal book of 2 Maccabees wrote to Jews exiled to Egypt, possibly as early as 163 B.C.[3] He envisioned a restored Israel regathered in a rebuilt and purified Temple (1:11,17; 2:17-18). To assure his readers that this restoration would be complete, he recounted for them how their fellow Egyptian exile, Jeremiah the prophet, had hidden the Temple treasures. In Maccabees 2:4-8 we learn that at the time of the destruction of the First Temple, Jeremiah took the Tabernacle, the incense altar, and the Ark to Mount Nebo and sealed them in a secret, unmarked cave. Since these vessels had their origin with Moses, keeping them "with him" at the site of his burial seemed fitting. The Greek word for "sealed" used here has prophetic meaning. It is the same word in the Greek translation of Daniel 12:4,9 (see 8:26), which speaks of a concealment until the end time. The author then has Jeremiah tell his followers that the Temple treasures would remain hidden until the time God regathered Israel and the glorious presence of God appeared in a cloud as at the exodus and

Solomon's dedication (Exodus 16:10; 1 Kings 8:11). Presumably, this would be at the rebuilt Temple in Jerusalem.

An anonymous medieval Jewish work called *Sepher Yosippon*, based on the work of Josephus, reports this same Jeremiah tradition. However, it adds that the secret spot would not be revealed until Jeremiah and Elijah came and returned the Ark to its place. This may combine the Jewish concept of the need for two witnesses with the prophetic figures of Jeremiah (who hid the vessels) and Elijah (who reveals all things). Some Jewish traditions thought of Elijah as a restorer of the Temple vessels.[4] He is clearly identified in this role in Mekhilta *Wayassa'* on Exodus 16:33-34: "And this is one of the three things which Elijah will, in the future restore to Israel; the bottle of sprinkling water [containing the ashes of the Red Heifer], and the bottle of anointing oil. And some say: Also the rod of Aaron with its ripe almonds and blossoms."

Two other legends concerning Jeremiah's hiding of Temple vessels also exist. In the *Life of Jeremiah* (11–19), the prophet takes only the Ark with its sacred contents to a secret place between Mount Nebo and Mount Hor and seals it within a rock. As in the Maccabees' story, the Ark will be brought out when Israel is regathered and the glory cloud appears. However, in this account the regathering is at Mount Sinai, and the resurrected Moses and Aaron will bring out the Ark. In a similar way in the *Paralipomena of Jeremiah* (3:5-19), Jeremiah (accompanied by Baruch) is commanded by God to take unspecified "holy vessels of the worship-service" and bury them. Again, they will only reappear at the time of the regathering. This account mentions that sacrificial worship will resume. Perhaps the author was drawing a connection between the reappearance of the Temple vessels and the restoration of Temple worship.

Baruch and the Hiding of the Temple Vessels

Another version of the hiding of the Temple treasure is that recorded in the Second Syriac *Apocalypse of Baruch* (6:5-9). In this account, Baruch witnesses an angel remove the Temple vessels before the Temple's destruction. Here the vessels include the Ark and its contents (the tablets of the law), the incense altar, the priests' clothing and 48 precious stones that were part of their raiment, the veil of the Temple, the ephod, and all the vessels of the Tabernacle. The angel then orders the earth to conceal them until the time of the restoration, when Jerusalem will be forever free (that is, the last days). One interesting note in this story is the explanation for the hiding of the vessels: "so that strangers may not get possession of them." This implies that only Jews and not Gentiles should be the ones to discover the treasures. In a slightly different Baruch tradition (4 Baruch), God tells Jeremiah to bury the Temple vessels "until the coming of the Beloved One." This messianic reference also places the restoration at the time of the end of days.

The Samaritans and the Hidden Temple Vessels

We find the Samaritan tradition concerning the hiding of the Temple vessels in Josephus' *Antiquities of the Jews* (18.85.88) and in the Samaritan chronicle called the *Memar Marqah*. The Samaritans were a non-Jewish people who were descendants of intermarriages between resident Israelites and Assyrian transplants after the exile of the northern kingdom (circa 669 B.C.). The Samaritans had attempted to disrupt the rebuilding of the Second Temple after the Jews rejected them from assisting in the project (Ezra 4:1-3). One reason for this rejection is that the Samaritans probably had their own temple on Mount Gerazim and did not want a rival Temple in Jerusalem (see John 4:20,25). Therefore, their offer to assist was in fact only a ruse.

However, the primary reason Zerubbabel could not allow them to participate was that they were foreigners whose religion was a mix of the Mosaic law and pagan beliefs. This very sort of religion had brought the destruction of the First Temple, and it would have threatened the unity of the Judeans and the work of God. The Samaritans did not have a part in the Jewish monarchy, so they did not accept any of the books of the Bible produced during this time. Consequently, they were left with only the Pentateuch (the first five books of the Old Testament). Therefore, the Samaritans developed a competitive version of the Temple treasure tradition based on Moses to support their own claim against Israel of being heir to the true (Mosaic only) worship.[5] The origin of their story, however, may have been influenced by an attempt to refute the charge of Genesis 35:2-4 that idols were hidden under Mount Gerazim.[6]

Understanding this, we are not surprised to find that in Josephus' Samaritan account, Moses is the one who buries the sacred vessels on Mount Gerazim. In this tradition, Moses does not appear at the end of days to recover them, but the prophet like Moses of Deuteronomy 18:15 (a messianic figure)[7] does at the time of the future ingathering of refugees at Mount Gerazim. According to the other Samaritan tradition in the *Memar Marqah* (4:11), Uzzi the high priest hides the Temple vessels at the beginning of the era of divine disfavor that is inaugurated by the death of Moses. Therefore, in both accounts, Moses or Moses' ultimate prophetic successor is responsible for hiding and restoring the Temple vessels.

Other Temple Treasure Traditions

The apocryphal book of Enoch records that the Tabernacle was folded up and buried in a secret place in the south and that it would be uncovered in a future age when the Messiah came to replace it with a new Temple (53:6; 91:13,28). Special items sometimes appear, as with Pseudo-Philo, who has God personally removing the Ark and its contents and storing it in an unknown place until God visits the earth and reveals the spot (26:12-15). In his Ark are the tablets, as expected, but also 12 sacred stones—presumably the gemstones that adorned the high priest's breastplate. Even the defiled stones of the altar were said to be stored under the Temple Mount until a prophet should arise to explain what should be done with them (1 Maccabees 4:46).

The Temple Scroll, the longest of the Dead Sea scrolls and the most detailed concerning the Temple, describes a restored future Temple, complete with all the original furnishings found in the Tabernacle and First Temple. Thus, either the Qumran community of the Qumran or the sects of Judaism in Jerusalem (depending on the theory of origin) looked forward to a recovery of the Ark and all the other vital vessels.

According to some Jewish writers, the Tabernacle, Ark, menorah, altar of incense, and other treasures were all stored within the First Temple and then concealed beneath the Temple when it was destroyed. Therefore, these vessels continued to remain intact and within the Temple throughout the Second Temple period. This is the popular rabbinic interpretation today, and supposedly it has been so whenever hopes of rebuilding the Temple have existed since A.D. 70. More will be said concerning this tradition in chapter 10.

These various accounts all reveal an early and long historical tradition concerning the Temple treasures. They all describe the hiding of at least the Ark and the end-time restoration of the vessels by God Himself or by a qualified prophetic representative.

Hidden Places of the Ark

Various traditions exist that place the Ark in one of several hiding places. The hiding place is secret, but it will be revealed in the last days. We will only briefly mention here the Irish legend of the Ark supposedly taken to these isles by Ollam Fodhla ("holy prophet") and a small band in 584 B.C.[8] According to this tradition of British Israelitism, the place in Ulster where this group landed was inhabited by descendants of the tribe of Daniel. The "holy prophet" who had brought the Ark was the prophet Jeremiah, and he subsequently buried it under a hill known today as Ollam Fodhla's Cairn (or Jeremiah's Cave). He had also brought the stone which Jacob used as a pillow, and this is claimed today to be the coronation stone fitted under the throne in Britain. This legend has no real historical support but is included because British Israelitism seems to be making a return among anti-Semitic groups in America and abroad.

We will consider two hiding places in detail, each with its own historical tradition. We will also evaluate whether the traditions have any real substance. These hiding places, quite different in historical affiliation, are the crypts of the Vatican and the chambers of the Temple Mount.

The Ark in the Vatican

The Arch of Titus' Triumph shows that the items captured from the Jewish Temple were taken to Rome. However, Rome's history from that time was quite turbulent, and once Christianity became the dominant religion of the empire, these treasures fell into the hands of the church. Historical records reveal that these treasures were in the possession of Pope Vitalian in A.D. 657. In recent years, Israeli emissaries to the Vatican have claimed that the menorah pictured on the Arch of Titus was deposited in church vaults in Rome, and they have asked the Pope for its return to the State of Israel. The Roman Church has continually denied that any such Jewish artifacts are in its possession.

Romans carry captured Temple vessels to Rome on the relief on the Arch of Titus' Triumph in the Roman Forum. Photo by author.

Nelson Canode of Amarillo, Texas, once served as a Benedictine monk at the monastery at Subiaco, Italy, 30 miles from Rome. He claimed to have seen Temple treasures. He says that he was taken to a room in a cave about four stories under the monastery. This room contained ancient artifacts that he assisted in moving back and forth from Subiaco to the underground vaults of the Vatican. When he asked his superiors what some of these things were, he was told they included the disassembled Tabernacle and the Ark.

Articles from the Second Temple were likely deposited in Rome. Josephus recorded that the emperor Vespasian had put some of the captured Temple treasures in a specially built "peace sanctuary" which he erected after the Jewish War to commemorate the Temple's destruction (*Wars of the Jews* 7:148-150). However, these items may not have been original treasures from the First Temple. The presence of the menorah and table of showbread on the Arch of Titus do not necessarily require this, for there were many duplicates of these objects kept in storage in the Temple treasuries in case the ones in service were defiled (see Talmud, *Haggai* 26b, 27a). One evidence that has led many Jewish scholars to believe that the menorah depicted on the arch was not the original is the picture of the menorah's octagonal base containing engraved images. Archaeological evidence of the earliest form of the menorah reveal a three-legged or triangular stand, not an octagonal base. These undoubtedly are patterned after the Mosaic model. Furthermore, Jewish menorot never possessed images, which were considered idolatrous (see Exodus 20:4; Deuteronomy 4:16-25; 5:8). This menorah was likely a non-Jewish creation, made by Herod's craftsmen as a gift to Rome. In support of this is the statement of Josephus that records priests giving to Titus "two lampstands similar to those deposited in the Temple" (*Wars of the Jews* 6.388). No priest would have been likely to hand over the holy menorah. And if this is true of the menorah, how much more would it be true of the untouchable Ark! In fact, no historical evidence exists that the Ark was among the Temple treasures taken by the Romans.

The story of Nelson Canode is fanciful, and the priest who told him what these articles were may have only been passing on a tradition or rumor. At any rate, nothing substantive supports a hiding of the Ark in the vaults in Rome.

We have seen in this chapter that the belief that the Ark was hidden in the past, rather than lost, stolen, or destroyed, has a long and somewhat sensational history. Yet it is precisely within history that the Ark has been hidden. If so, history should have much more to reveal about the Ark. It does indeed, and I invite you to continue searching throughout history with me, particularly the history of the ancient Temple, for new clues to uncovering the hiding place of the Ark.

9
Hidden Within History

All your life has been spent in pursuit of archaeological
relics. Inside the Ark are treasures beyond your wildest
aspirations. You want to see it opened as well as I.
Indiana, we are simply passing *through* history.
This, this *is* history!

—Rene Belloq to Indiana Jones
Raiders of the Lost Ark

We have examined numerous proposals for where the Ark may have been hidden in the past. We have seen that these accounts have important similarities. In each, the Ark is hidden and will be revealed in the end time, either by God or by His representative. Now let us consider the biblical data as to the importance of the Temple treasures and the prospect for their future recovery.

The Treasures and the Temple

The Temple vessels were an essential part of the Temple, made according to God's specific command and pattern (Exodus 25:9; 1 Chronicles 28:11-19). These vessels were considered holy and a vital part of the worship of God. Israel's conqueror demonstrated his superior power by placing the Temple vessels in his own temple. This event plays an important role in the drama of Daniel as the vessels put in the Babylonian temple (1:2) become the focal point of God demonstrating His sovereignty over Babylon. The desecration of the vessels by Belshazzar (5:1-4) appears as a pagan gauntlet thrown in the face of Israel's God. As a result, God, who had declared that "all the nations will know that I am the LORD" (see Ezekiel 36:23), immediately brought about the complete overthrow of the nation of Babylon (5:25-31).

The Return of the Temple Treasures

This account of the Temple vessels in Babylon underscores their tremendous sanctity. Any violation of this sanctity or common use of the chambers where they were stored was a grave offense (see Nehemiah 13:4-9). To this end they were continually purified (2 Chronicles 29:18) and guarded (1 Chronicles 9:28) to ensure that the Temple service would not be interrupted. When the First Temple was destroyed, these vessels of necessity had to be recovered or remade before the Temple could be rebuilt (Ezra 1:7-11; 3:10-11; 5:14-15; 6:5). At this time we read of the expectation of the recovery of one of the Temple treasures—the Urim and Thummim (Ezra 2:63)—devices used to discern the will of God. We also read of the acquisition of other treasures for the Temple (Ezra 7:14-20; 8:25-34). These, however, were not vessels for worship but wealth for the Temple treasury.

The Link with the Temple

The items used within the Temple itself (not the Temple treasury) were vitally connected to the Temple's existence. In fact, although the Temple had been desecrated by foreign idols (Jeremiah 7; Ezekiel 8) and its treasury plundered prior to the Babylonian destruction (2 Kings 24:13), the climactic event spelling the doom of all Jerusalem was the removal of the choicest of the Temple vessels (2 Chronicles 36:18-19).[1] This passage reveals that the Temple and its vessels are inseparable. Therefore, the destiny of the two must be prophetically linked as well. This idea is also witnessed outside the biblical canon by the pseudepigraphical work 2 Baruch, which appears to suggest that the recovered vessels provide a continuity between the destruction of the Temple and its restoration.

Therefore, just as the Temple was destroyed by the Babylonians, and a second time by the Romans, according to the word of God (Jeremiah 7:14; Luke 21:5-6,20-24), so too were the Temple vessels (2 Kings 24:13; Jeremiah 27:16-22). Yet the Temple was, and is, to be rebuilt by God's word (see Daniel 9:16-17,20-27), and so also these treasures will be restored. Jeremiah 27:22 supports this deduction: " 'They will be carried to Babylon, and they shall be there until the day I visit them,' declares the LORD. 'Then I will bring them back and restore them to this place.' " Isaiah 52:11-12 similarly predicted this restoration of the vessels but stated more clearly the idea of divine preservation, which Jeremiah had only implied: "Depart, depart, go out from there...you who carry the vessels of the LORD. But you will not go out in haste, nor will you go as fugitives; for the LORD will go before you, and the God of Israel will be your rear guard."

These words refer to the first return of the Jewish people and the first restoration of the Temple (Jeremiah 28:1-6), but they set a pattern for the predicted second Jewish return (Isaiah 11:11; Ezekiel 36:24-28) and restoration of the Temple (Ezekiel 37:26-28; 40–48; Daniel 9:27; Zechariah 6:12-15; Matthew 24:15; 2 Thessalonians 2:4; Revelation 11:1-2). Just as Jeremiah and Isaiah predicted the overthrow of Babylon and the restoration of Israel in the past, so John predicts the same for the future (Revelation 17–20). If the first destruction of 586 B.C. was reversed, must not the second of A.D. 70 as surely be reversed? If the vessels were part of the Second Temple, should they not be a part of the Third? If, as the Jeremiah text implies, the future of the vessels is connected with the future of the Jewish people in the land of Israel, then we should be able to give an affirmative answer to these questions.

The detailed lists of Temple vessels that were captured imply the promise of their restoration (see 2 Kings 25:13-17). If the vessels were to be destroyed and forgotten, then why preserve them in such detail? The same has been argued for the Temple, whose precise measurements have been passed down in such works as Josephus and the Mishnah tractate known as *Middot* ("measurements").

The Ark in the Dead Sea Scrolls

The longest of the Dead Sea Scrolls is known as the Temple Scroll because of its description of a new Temple to be built by a restored Israel. It states that the Temple will contain the Ark of the Covenant. The reference comes in the instructions to construct a set of overshadowing cherubim as were present in the First Temple.

> And two cherubim [you shall make at both ends of the cover, the one cherub on this end, and the othe]r end the second, spreading (their) wings [over the place of the ark, and shielding the cover with their wings] above the ark, with their faces on[e to the other] (11Q19 7:10-12).

If this Temple was to be legitimate it must include the Ark, as did the Tabernacle in the wilderness and the First Temple, for only with the Ark present could the glory of God return to take its appointed place between the wings of the cherubim (see

Ezekiel 43:1-7). The Temple Scroll seems to have understood that the restoration Temple would at least include the elements of the Tabernacle and the First Temple (see Haggai 2:3-9). The rabbis noted that five things[2] from the First Temple were missing from the Second Temple, including the Ark (Mishnah tractates *Seqalim* 6:1-2 and *Yoma* 5:2; Tosefta tractates *Yoma* 3:14 and *Sota* 13:1; Babylonian Talmud tractate *Yoma* 21b; see *Jewish Wars* 5.5.5). The author of the Temple Scroll felt that only the pattern of the Tabernacle would suffice for his Temple, since he probably regarded the First Temple as having been improperly built, and the Second Temple, aside from being polluted, contained no Ark. This fact was emphasized in the extrabiblical literature (see 2 Maccabees 2:4-5; 2 Apocalypse of Baruch 6:7-10) but only as a means to heighten the Ark's return as a sign of the messianic age. In part, for the same reason the Temple Scroll's author would have included the Ark.

If the Ark of the Covenant disappeared with the destruction of the First Temple, and was not present in the Second Temple, from where would those who were to construct this new Temple expect to recover it? The answer undoubtedly is in the Jewish traditions concerning the hidden Temple vessels. These traditions began sometime shortly after the return from exile and were included in the apocryphal and pseudepigraphal literature that arose in the postexilic period, about the same time as the movement that produced the Scrolls. This same tradition may have also influenced those who later hid the treasures of the Copper Scroll. The traditions themselves may go back to the texts in 2 Chronicles 35:3, which the rabbis later interpreted as implying a hiding place for the Ark, and Jeremiah 3:16-17, the only text that relates to both the Ark's disappearance and Jerusalem's future restoration. The author of the Temple Scroll did not base his new Temple on

Ezekiel's plan, but he may have been informed by Ezekiel's indirect statement of the Ark's return to the future Temple in Ezekiel 43:1-7. The Jewish versions of the tradition all tell of the Ark hidden away safely and secretly (either by men or by angels) within the Temple precincts (usually in a subterranean chamber beneath the Holy of Holies).[3] The information concerning the actual location of the Ark was said to have been entrusted to one priestly Zadokite family, and this may have been conveyed to the author of the Temple Scroll. If so, the Jews would assume that when they took possession of Jerusalem and the Temple Mount and restored its sanctity, they would also be able to restore the Ark to the new Temple.

The Tabernacle in the Temple

When Israel dedicated the First Temple, the Levites "brought up the ark of the LORD and the tent of meeting and all the holy utensils, which were in the tent" (1 Kings 8:4) and carried them "into the inner sanctuary of the house, to the holy of holies" (2 Chronicles 5:7). A careful comparison of the measurements of the Tabernacle with a certain space inside the Holy of Holies in the Temple reveals an interesting correspondence. Richard Friedman is a scholar who has studied this relationship, and he makes this observation:

> According to the description of the Temple construction (1 Kings 6; 2 Chronicles 3) the Holy of Holies (or *debir*) is 20 cubits in length and 20 cubits in width (1 Kgs 6:20; 2 Chr. 3:8). Within are the two cherubim, each 10 cubits high. Their wings are spread and the wingspread of each is 10 cubits, so that the tips of the wings of each touch the walls of the room

> on each side and touch each other in the center of the room (1 Kgs 6:23-27; 2 Chr 3:10-13). Thus the space between the cherubims is 10 cubits in height, 20 cubits in length, and less than 10 cubits in width (as the bodies of the cherubim take up a portion of the center space). The measurements of the Tabernacle, as pictured in Exodus 26 and 36, are just this: 10 cubits in height, 20 cubits in length, and 8 cubits in width.

This arrangement may only represent a *symbolic* spatial correspondence between the Tabernacle and the Holy of Holies. The Tabernacle was the ordained place of sacrifice (see 2 Chronicles 1:3-4), and therefore it properly had to be included within the Temple's construction, even if only symbolically. However the scriptural texts and extrabiblical literature allow for the possibility that the actual Tabernacle was placed within the Temple.

The Tabernacle Beneath the Temple

In order for us to understand the meaning of these descriptions of the Tabernacle being in the Temple, we must realize that the Tabernacle and the tent of meeting were in fact one single structure composed of two separate parts. According to Numbers 3:25 the inner fabric of this structure was called in Hebrew the *mishkan* ("Tabernacle"), and the outer fabric was referred to as the *'ohel* ("tent"). The relationship between these two parts was conveyed in the biblical text through a literary device known as hendiadys, a pairing of terms to express one unified thought. Therefore, 1 Chronicles 6:32 can refer to "the tabernacle of the tent of meeting," and 2 Samuel 7:6 speaks of God "moving about in a tent, even in a Tabernacle."

When we examine the book of Chronicles in particular, we find that the Temple is referred to as "the house of the tent" (2 Chronicles 9:23). In the Psalms, the Tabernacle is likewise pictured within the Temple precincts. For instance, Psalm 74:7, a verse lamenting the destruction of the Temple in 586 B.C., literally reads: "They cast Your temple into the fire; they profaned Your name's tabernacle." Psalm 61:4 may allude to the Tabernacle's spatial relationship to the Ark: "Let me dwell in Your tent forever; let me take refuge in the shelter of Your wings" [that is, of the cherubim].

The extrabiblical writers explain why the Tabernacle is set within the Temple. Josephus states that the Tabernacle was brought into the First Temple (*Antiquities* 8.101.106) and that the spread-winged cherubim were designed to appear as a tent (8.103). Rabbinic tradition further asserts that the tent of meeting was stored away in the subterranean vault beneath the Holy of Holies (see Babylonian Talmud, *Sota* 9a; *Yoma* 21b; Rashi on Genesis 9:27). Friedman again interprets this for us:

> It is possible that the Tabernacle was in fact stored in the manner which the Talmud describes, while the appropriately measured space beneath the wings of the cherubim meanwhile corresponded to it above.[4]

What this means is that the Tabernacle was deposited in the chamber Solomon constructed to house the Temple treasures. Directly above it, in the Holy of Holies, the Tabernacle was represented at the Ark. Some have even argued that the inner tent of the Tabernacle was physically present with the Ark, appearing in the form of the dividing or covering curtain known as the *paroket*. The idea by this arrangement may have been to testify to the immanence of God with the Ark and the Tabernacle, and to the transcendence of God with the tent. This reveals that the Jews believed the prior sanctity of a structure can continue to sanctify whatever contains it, in this case the Temple. Therefore, just as the Tabernacle was present beneath the First Temple, yet continued to provide a sanctity to the Holy of Holies above it, so in the Second Temple, when the Ark joined the tent of meeting in the secret chamber, it too could provide this function for the empty Holy of Holies. This, then, suggests the existence of a hiding place for the Ark when such became necessary. Later Judaism describes such a repository.

The Ark in the Temple Mount Chambers

Jewish tradition held that the Ark continued in existence and that it would be rediscovered and restored to Israel when the Messiah appeared. Contrary to apocryphal sources that had the Ark hidden at Mount Sinai or Mount Nebo, the Ark was only and always hidden under the Temple Mount. According to the Mishnah (*Sotah* 9a), the Tabernacle had been stored under the Temple Mount in a subterranean chamber: "With regard to Moses the Master said: 'After the First Temple was erected, the Tent of Meeting was stored away, its boards, hooks, bars, pillars, and sockets.' Where [were they stored]? Rabbi Hisda said in the name of Abimi: 'Beneath the crypts of the Temple.' "

Jewish tradition held that along with the Tabernacle, the Ark, the incense altar, Aaron's rod, the pot of manna, and the tablets of the law were all hidden within a secret compartment beneath the pen of wood or woodshed on the west side of the Temple, close to the Holy of Holies.[5] This spot on the Temple Mount was considered so sacred that it affected the normal pattern of worship for those who knew and accepted its secret. It was the regular custom of the priests to bow at 13 stations in the Temple.

But members of the house of Rabbi Gamaliel and of the deputy high priest, Rabbi Hananiah, used to bow at 14. This additional place was facing the woodshed. The sources say that they did this because they had inherited from their ancestors the secret that this was the place where the Ark was hidden.[6] All others who did not know of this tradition believed that the Ark had been taken to Babylon, and so they only observed the 13 locations.[7]

Since these vessels were kept with the Ark in the Temple, when the Ark disappeared, so did these other vessels. This, at least, is consistent with the historical record. However, what about this tradition of the hiding of the Ark? Let us consider whether there exists any basis in history and in fact for this tradition.

The Historical Basis for the Legend

This tradition maintains that when King Solomon built the Temple, he foresaw its eventual destruction and built a secret chamber deep within the Temple Mount to conceal the Temple treasures at such a time of danger. The biblical text records that such a threat was present—the Egyptian pharaoh Shishak plundered the Temple treasury soon after Solomon's death (1 Kings 14:25-26). Later, during the dark days of the kings Manasseh and Amon, who desecrated the Temple with abominable images, the Ark, as well as the other primary Temple treasures, must have been removed to this chamber for safekeeping. The reason for this is that Manasseh's pollution of the Temple, with the corresponding cessation of the Temple ritual, would have demanded the Temple priests and Levites go into hiding. That they should not take with them the holy Ark, committed to their care, would be unthinkable.

The rabbis concluded that the apostasy in Israel during the reigns of Manasseh and Amon was too deep-seated to be completely reversed by Josiah's reforms. Consequently, when Josiah died, the nation returned to its sin and merited divine punishment. Therefore, the rabbis held that when Josiah made extensive repairs to the Temple (2 Kings 22:5-6), he decided that he must hide the Ark for safekeeping because he believed the prophecies of destruction were true and would shortly come to pass. As part of his religious reforms, he reinstituted the priestly service and commanded the Ark to be returned to the Temple. In 2 Chronicles 35:3 we read, "Put the holy ark in the house which Solomon the son of David king of Israel built; it will be a burden on your shoulders no longer."

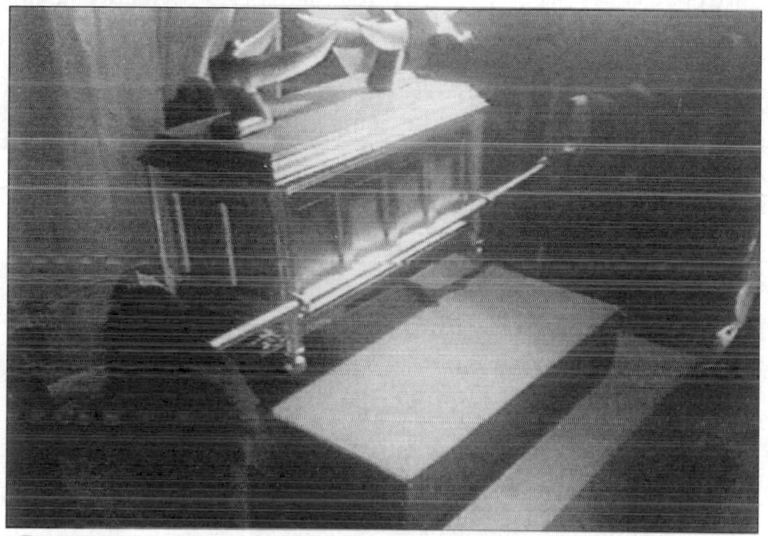

Recreation of the hiding of the Ark beneath the Temple Mount by priests before the Babylonian invasion. Courtesy Desperado Films and Sun International Pictures.

The rabbis took sides in their commentaries on the last part of this verse, some arguing that this implied that the Ark was hidden in a secret chamber not only in those days but also during the Babylonian invasion, and thus was preserved (*Yoma* 52b). What else could this verse mean but that the Ark had been deposited in a subterranean chamber of the Temple? Where else could the Ark have been during the years in between? How else could the Ark have remained free from defilement in the presence of a defiled Temple?

The rabbis, however, interpreted the command of Josiah to mean that the Levites were to put the Ark back in the subterranean chamber. They argued that the Ark had *always* been in the Temple, so how could it be put back? Yet, if this were what Josiah meant, why did he say it should be taken *in* the "house which Solomon built"? The rabbis had an answer for this. This answer was that the Temple to which the Ark was taken was a *different* Temple from where it had been. The explanation for this is that the Ark had to have been removed from the First Temple in order for God's prophecy of the Temple's destruction to have been fulfilled by the Babylonians. As long as the Ark remained, they saw the Temple as invulnerable to attack. But once it was removed to the underground labyrinth of passageways below the Temple, the upper part of the Temple became simply an outer shell, devoid of all sanctity. Thus, it was able to be destroyed. What this meant was that the true "house of Solomon" now existed in the vaulted region beneath the Temple. Therefore the command to return the Ark to the "house which Solomon built" meant this subterranean house.[8] Other elaborate argumentation also exists among the rabbis in support of this view.[9]

According to Jewish thought, the Ark remained through the entire time of the Second Temple under Zerubbabel and its enlargement under King Herod. The fifth division of the tractate *Mo'ed* in the Mishnah, called *Yoma,* records the absence of the Ark when it explains that because the Ark had been removed from the Second Temple, the high priest made his offering instead upon an ancient rock that protruded through the floor within the Holy of Holies called the "foundation stone" (Hebrew *'even hashtiyah*). It was around this stone, the highest point of Mount Moriah, that Abraham had offered Isaac and later King David had seen the angelic destroyer of Jerusalem on the threshing floor of Araunah the Jebusite.

The historical and religious context in which the Second Temple existed shows why the Ark could not have been returned to it. During the time of Zerubbabel, Judah was under the hegemony of Persia, and under Herod it was occupied by Rome. During both periods the Temple was never totally free from the threat of attack. In fact, Rome had placed their eagle insignia above the eastern (Shushan) gate of the Temple, and Romans made various attempts to set standards bearing images of the emperor in the Temple precincts. In addition, many Jewish sects felt that a non-Zadokite priesthood in specific, and the political corruption of the high priesthood in general, had brought desecration to the Herodian Temple. There was even a popular opinion that held that the Second Temple was to be imminently destroyed in order to make room for God's final and purified Restoration Temple. Under these conditions, no Levite who knew the secret of the Ark would have revealed it, nor would he have considered returning the Ark to its foundation stone platform within the Holy of Holies.

The Ark had certainly not been returned to the Temple, for when the Roman general Pompey invaded Jerusalem in A.D. 63, he entered the Holy of Holies and found it completely empty.[10] He thought the Jewish Temple would house great treasure because the Jews protested his entrance at the offer of their own lives. However, if they believed the Ark was hidden beneath the Holy of Holies, the Temple would have continued to retain its sanctity, and it would have been worthy of their sacrifice. Such a regard for the Temple Mount persists among Jews today based on this same thinking. Rabbi Aryeh Kaplan explains:

> Even today, it is possible to experience this feeling of proximity. These most sacred objects still remain hidden in Jerusalem, buried deep in a vault under the Temple Mount. Here they will remain until the time when we are worthy to uncover them once again. And even though we may not actually be aware of these sacred objects, the very fact of their proximity is sure to make a most profound impression on our souls.[11]

An Ancient Account of the Hidden Ark

An account in the Mishnah revealed the secret where the Ark was hidden while at the same time indirectly giving a warning to those who might seek for it. Tractate *Shekalim* 6:1-2 (see *Yoma* 52a-54a) records that a priest during Second Temple times was in the "wood store," separating the good wood from the bad (wormy) wood for the sacrificial altar. As he was working he noticed that some of the stones in the floor of the room were different from the other stones. This was interpreted by the rabbis to mean that a certain flagstone was higher than the rest, and he surmised that this stone had once been removed and then replaced in order to hide the Ark. When he went to tell his fellow priest that he had discovered the secret chamber of the Ark (which apparently was entered from the "wood store"), he was struck dead in mid sentence, thus definitely confirming that the place was the repository of the Ark. One of the rabbis (Rivevan) explained that the reason the priest was struck down was because if the secret were known, Gentiles might learn this information and seize the Ark.

The Archaeological Support for the Theory

Talmud *Yoma* 54a argues on the basis of this story in *Shekalim* that it proved that when Nebuchadnezzar destroyed the Temple, he left the foundational pavement intact. Although the Temple Mount has been inaccessible for excavation because of almost 2000 years of foreign occupation, such accounts preserved in the Mishnah have kept Orthodox rabbis confident of the Ark's existence beneath the Temple platform. Since the return of East Jerusalem and the Temple Mount to Jewish control, explorers claim to now be able to confirm not only that the foundational pavement was left intact but also where the "wood store" or "pen of wood" and the hidden chamber of the Ark are located!

Evidence of the Temple Mount's subterranean passageways was originally gathered from early British exploration maps. After the Israeli capture of the Temple Mount in the Six-Day War of 1967, a corps of army engineers under the authority of then Israel Defense Forces Chaplain Rabbi Shlomo Goren also conducted some hasty surveys. Furthermore, excavations in the Western Wall Tunnel over the past 15 years have confirmed the presence of the foundational pavement and have uncovered one of the original ancient entrances to the Temple Mount, now known as Warren's Gate. Excavations from this gate in the direction of the Holy of Holies claim to have discovered a tunnel leading to a chamber 48 feet below the present surface of the platform in an area called the *Gear Ha'Etzem* ("Chalk of the Bone"). This location matches exactly the description given in the traditional sources of the secret repository of the Ark and other Temple treasures, but I will leave the details of this excavation for the next chapter. On the basis of our survey in this chapter, we may conclude that if the Ark is in hiding in any place, that place would have to be the Temple Mount. It is time for us to leave our studies and our surveys and make an exploration of our own in a tunnel deep beneath the streets of Old Jerusalem. There we will join with traditional rabbis and excavators sworn to secrecy as we search for an answer to the question, Is the Ark under the Temple Mount?

Subterranean passageway known as the Western Wall Tunnel that priests of the Second Temple used to enter the gate closest to the Holy of Holies. Photo by Paul Streber.

10

Is the Ark Under the Temple Mount?

The looting of the Temple and its destruction by fire which followed the second Babylonian Conquest of 586 B.C. would have revealed any hiding place which existed above ground level on the Mount. But the Temple Mount offers the ideal place of concealment for the Ark underground. If it was hidden underground it could have remained in its hiding place, protected from the ravages of war and preserved for posterity.[1]

—Richard Andrews

The historical accounts support the Jewish tradition that the Ark is presently hidden beneath the Temple Mount. If it was indeed stored away in the past—and has not yet been removed from its hiding place—then it must still remain under the Temple Mount today. Dr. Dan Bahat, former District Archaeologist for Jerusalem and present Archaeological Supervisor for the Western Wall Tunnels, once stated that he did not believe the Ark of the Covenant could have survived the Babylonian destruction. Today, however, he has stated that he believes the Ark may be under the Temple Mount.[2] If such a renowned archaeologist as this can change his mind concerning the destiny of the Ark, perhaps you too are willing to consider the evidence and the claims of those who do believe. But to begin, we must understand the controversial conditions on the Temple Mount, which for 1300 years, and especially in the past 40 years, have elevated the risks and the urgency of searching for the Ark.

The Temple Mount Today

With the capture of the Temple Mount by Israeli forces in 1967 and the subsequent exercise of sovereignty over the site, we might assume that Jewish religious authorities would have instigated a search for the Ark. However, while the Temple Mount has been under the sovereignty of the State of Israel, Israelis have never exercised sovereignty there. Part of the reason is that the same traditional history that argues for the Ark's existence under the Temple Mount also argues against any Jew setting foot within the sacred compound. Orthodox Jewry has always maintained that the Temple Mount is off limits because ceremonial law states that all Jews have incurred ritual defilement, and only those who have been ritually purified can enter. From their perspective, the presence of the Lord still attends the Ark, and since it is buried somewhere beneath the surface of the Temple Mount, no observant Jew could walk there without inadvertently transgressing by defiling the Holy Place. The only means of purification to enable one to enter—the ashes of the red heifer (Numbers 19)—have been lost for 2000 years, and no qualified red heifers are said to exist today in the land of Israel. Therefore, the present rabbinate contends, until the Messiah appears and declares the exact location of the Holy of Holies, Jews cannot enter the site.

Despite this ruling of the rabbinate, some Jewish authorities believe the exact location of the Holy of Holies can be known today, and they have launched their own search under the Temple Mount to locate the Ark. But before we consider their story, let us understand the modern background of the Temple Mount, which has made them confident of the location of the Holy Place and has allowed them to contravene Jewish religious law in pursuit of the hidden Ark. Let us begin with the tragedy of the Temple Mount, an event that returned the jurisdiction of the site to the Muslim authorities shortly after its coming under Israeli control in 1967.

The Tragedy of the Temple Mount

In 1967, many Jews experienced feelings of tragedy and betrayal as Defense Minister Moshe Dayan removed the Jewish jurisdiction of Judaism's most holy site from the control of Rabbi Shlomo Goren and returned it to the Wakf (the Islamic Trust having administration over Islamic holy sites). It had been captured from Jordanian forces only a month earlier during the final days of the Six Day War. A jubilant Israeli army occupied the site and hoisted the flag of the State of Israel to the top of the Dome of the Rock. The Arab world, with the world at large, expected to soon see the erection of the long-awaited Jewish Temple. Rabbi Shlomo Goren, then Chaplain of the Israel Defense Forces, but later to become the Chief Ashkenazi Rabbi of Israel, was placed in charge of the Temple Mount, and he immediately assigned a corps of engineers a two-week task of measuring and mapping the area. He also opened a synagogue on the Mount and brought Torah scrolls, prayer books, and other items of worship in expectation of a revival of Jewish presence at the site. But after only one month, Dayan ordered him to close down the synagogue and evacuate the site, announcing that Israel had given it back to the Muslims as a gesture of peace. Rabbi Goren explains the exceptional nature of this act and of his feelings on that day:

> I had a fight with Dayan for us to remain on the Temple Mount. But Dayan was pro-Arabic, and religion was meaningless to him and the Temple Mount was unimportant to him. I said to him, "Who gave you permission to hand over the Temple Mount—the Holy of the Holies of Israel—to them [the Arabs]?" He said, "This is the decision of the government!" It was not true. He acted [on his own authority] and the government accepted whatever he did.[3]

Dayan may have believed that many religious Jews, including Rabbi Goren himself, intended to destroy the Islamic structures on the Mount and prepare for the rebuilding of the Third Temple. Dayan considered a Jewish occupation of the Temple Mount as a provocation that would only lead to a greater war with the Arab world, and so he took the initiative that has since taken center stage in the Arab-Israeli conflict. Despite what he felt was a betrayal of the Jewish nation on the eve of the messianic era, Rabbi Goren decided to wait for a more suitable occasion to explore the Mount. His patience would endure almost two decades until late one night in July 1981 a surprise phone call from another rabbi presented the opportunity he had long awaited.

The Rabbi's Story

The excited phone call came from Rabbi Meir Yehuda Getz, Chief Rabbi of the Holy Places in Israel. In the process of clearing an area inside the Western Wall Tunnel to construct the closest synagogue to the Temple Mount in recent history, his workmen had revealed the arch of one of the ancient gates to the Temple Mount more than 2000 years old. This gate had been discovered a century earlier by the British explorer Charles

Warren during the first probes ever attempted underground at the Temple Mount. However, its exact location had not been preserved clearly in Warren's excavation reports, and Warren never revealed how he had found it or how he knew it to be one of the four ancient entrance gates to the Temple mentioned by Josephus. It was rediscovered and identified by the British explorer and excavator Charles Wilson (who named it "Warren's Gate") beneath the obscure Gate *Bab-el-Mat'hara,* which had been used as an Arab latrine until 1967. The vaulted passageway within was partially used as a water reservoir or cistern up until recent times. Historical sources tell us that this gate led directly onto the Temple courts and was used for bringing in wood, sacrifices, and other materials needed for the Temple rites. Dr. Dan Bahat notes the historical significance of this site:

> This [gate] is a threshold to the Temple Mount and...one of the gates to the Temple. This gate is the most important of all the gates because it is the nearest gate to the Holy of Holies. The eastern extremity of this passage is even nearer to the Holy of Holies, and this is why it was preferable for Jews to pray inside this vault. For over 450 years it was the holiest place where people came to pray, or in other words, from the Arab conquest of 638 A.D. till the Crusader conquest of 1099 A.D., it was the central synagogue of Israel's Jewry. It was called the Cave because it has the form of a cave, a kind of an underground vault penetrating into the

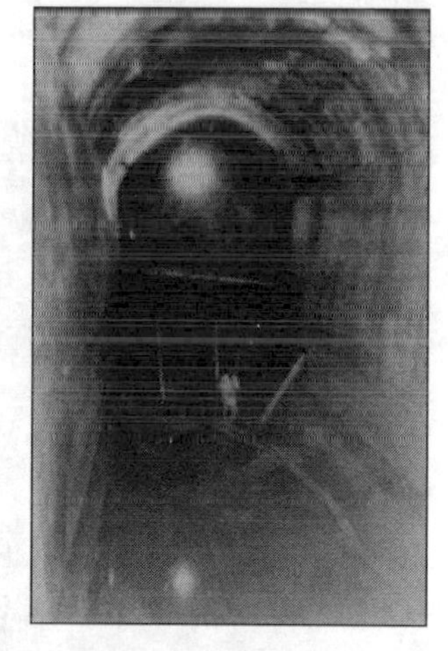

Temple Mount, and thus it played a very important role in Jewish life in Jerusalem in the early Arab period simply because of its proximity to the Holy of Holies. When the Jews returned to Jerusalem after

The author and the late Rabbi Shlomo Goren,
former Chief Rabbi of Israel, who governed the Temple Mount in 1967.

The author and the late Rabbi Meir Yehuda Getz,
Chief Rabbi of the Western Wall and Holy Places in Israel.

> the Crusader rule, the Jews wanted to come back into [Warren's Gate], but the whole area was filled in with Islamic buildings, so they chose the second best site, the Western Wall farther down [from the site of the Temple].[4]

This account by Bahat testifies to the sanctity accorded to this area in previous centuries, a sanctity that may well have been attached to the site because of its proximity to the place mentioned in traditional Jewish sources as the hiding place of the Ark. Josephus tells us this gate, the most direct access to the Temple from the west, may have connected with other subterranean passageways officiating priests in the Temple used to reach *miqvahs* (ritual purification pools) located both north and south of the Temple complex. If so, the gate might have also connected with a tunnel that entered the hidden passageway that led from under the "wood store" (mentioned in Mishnah tractate *Shekalim* 6:1-2) to the chamber of the Ark.

Returning to our story, Rabbi Getz had instructed his workers to knock out a place in the stone wall to affix a Torah cabinet. In doing so, they accidentally reopened the entrance to Warren's Gate. After receiving the call about the discovery, Rabbi Goren decided to secretly remove the debris that filled the gate and try to reach the place of the Ark. He eventually gathered together ten men, including students of the Ateret Cohanim Yeshiva, whom he swore to secrecy. They worked late at night inside the newly opened passageway for more than a year and a half. As Rabbi Goren declared, "Nobody on the outside knew what we were doing inside. No news of our dig had been revealed to any journalist; we did not reveal the story to anyone. We had a budget, and only a few people—about ten—were engaged in the work, but they took a vow not to tell anything about their work."[5] After

Rabbi Getz' workmen opened the gate, Rabbi Goren explored it and came to the conviction that this entrance led toward the Ark:

> After we traced the leaking water to its source, we discovered this large opening [Warren's Gate] 25 meters long, 30 meters high, and 8 meters wide. [I believed] it was from the First Temple. When we found this entrance [gate], I ordered the wall to be opened, and we discovered a giant hall shaped like the Wilson Arch but with exit tunnels running in different directions. The length [of this hall] was about 75 feet. There were some stairs that we descended for about 30 feet; however, at the bottom everything was full of water and mud. When we pumped this away I found an insect. This insect verified that this place was the place opposite the Holy of Holies [because] it is recorded in [the Mishnah] tractate *Yoma* that if the priest was found unclean, and therefore unable to get out of the Holy of Holies, [he] should release an insect that would go under the veil. I have discovered this insect![6]

Once the two rabbis realized the opportunity before them of actually entering the secret priestly passageways hidden for 2500 years, they began clearing the great hall inside the gate that once had served as a cistern to the Mount. Behind this room the team began work on one of the passageways that led to the northeast. Rabbi Getz continued: "From [the place where the insect was discovered] we saw several openings. One entrance was toward the gate. It was closed, but we opened it. From there we saw a wall that was later built and was about nine to twelve feet away from the warning wall of the western wall, which itself was only fifteen feet from the Holy of Holies."[7] The excavators then proceeded onward in the direction of the Holy of Holies underneath which they believed lay the chamber of the Ark. Rabbi Goren recounted this dramatic point in the excavation: "We were very close to the place on the Temple Mount where the Holy of the Holies was located. We were very close, beneath the Holy of the Holies. We believe that the holy Ark made by Moses, and the table from the Temple, and the candelabra made by Moses, along with other very important items, are hidden very deep underneath the Holy of the Holies. We started digging and we came close to the place; we were not more than 30 or 40 yards away."[8]

The Secret Shattered

Although the excavation of the tunnel had been a carefully guarded secret, it could not remain so forever. One reporter learned of the clandestine late-night work and went to Rabbi Goren with his suspicions. Although he begged him not to reveal the story, the reporter eventually announced the news on a radio broadcast. When word came to the Wakf (who control the Temple Mount) that the rabbis were about to uncover the Ark, the Wakf stopped the excavations by calling a general strike, staging a riot, and sending a Muslim mob to attack the excavators. Chaim Richman of the Temple Institute, who accompanied me at one of my interviews with Rabbi Getz concerning this story, suggests that the Wakf had definite motives for the attack:

> They were afraid that if the Jews found these objects that it would be the surest sign of all of a Jewish presence on the Temple Mount. It wasn't some sort of mystical tradition. They were afraid that if these things were uncovered that we would rebuild the Temple. [It is part of] an orchestrated effort to destroy and eradicate any semblance of Jewish presence around the Temple Mount.[9]

Rabbi Goren claimed that the entire riot scenario was part of a political conspiracy to close his diggings in deference to Arab sensitivities following the Camp David peace accord between Israel and Egypt.

Gershon Salomon, who was part of the excavation team, related to me what happened inside the tunnel:

> We had just discovered another wall, which blocked our continuance [into the tunnel]. I remember that the workers, along with Rabbi Getz, started to break down this wall, since beyond this point [Rabbi Getz conjectured] it continued to the place under the floors where the Ark of the Covenant, the menorah, and the other vessels were. We were so very, very close! [But] at this moment the Arabs started to demonstrate against our activities.[10]

Meanwhile, on the outside Rabbi Goren tells the story of his fight with government officials whom he first thought would protect the excavation, only to again feel betrayed as they arrested his workmen and sought to close the project:

> After he [the newsman] announced it, the Arabs got together on the Temple Mount and prepared to open the entrances [on the Temple Mount] to go down [inside the tunnels] and prevent our work. But while they [the Arabs] were still talking about it, Joseph Berg, the Minister of the Interior and of the police, suddenly came to me at my office and said that he would like to prevent the Arabs from going down to stop our work. He promised to put police at every entrance on the Temple Mount and [in addition] to

put an iron chain on the opening of these entrances so that no one could go down. But I didn't trust him. I knew that Berg would, if he could, hand over the Temple Mount to the Arabs—to the Wakf. So I asked him to sign an agreement, which he did, but before he had even left the building on the elevator I got a call from the [Western] Wall saying: Did you know that there is a fight at the Wall with your people where they are digging? There are hundreds of Arabs that have gone down into the chambers and there could be bloodshed! I knew then that Berg had cooked [concocted] the story to camouflage his real act of opening the entrances to the Arabs and telling them to go down to get us.

When I arrived at the Wall there were hundreds of police—even the chief of police—and I was happy that they were there because they [the Arabs] would not be able to do anything. I asked them to come with me to see what was going on inside the dig. Some of the top officers followed me, and when I reached the place there were hundreds of Arabs inside—coming in from both sides—and crying and shouting. Rabbi Getz was also inside with me, so I went to get the police to arrest the Arabs and take them out, but when I turned all of the officers had disappeared. When I came outside [of the tunnel] to the Wall there were no police to be found. There are always police at the Wall to protect the people—to be on the safe side, but this time there were none! I became afraid because we were alone, so I called Berg at his office and told him that he had betrayed me! I asked him to send the

> police to protect us because otherwise we would be killed. When the police could not be found, I called him again and told him he would be responsible and that I was going to mobilize the boys of the Yeshivat ha Kotel and my Yeshiva, and they were going down with pistols—with weapons—and there will be bloodshed. So I called to General Ariel Sharon, the Defense Minister, and told him the story and said if you do not send soldiers to evacuate the Arabs from the chambers there will be bloodshed. But he said that he had foreign guests and could not do anything.
>
> Finally, I called to the boys from the Yeshiva and a few hundred came with weapons. Meanwhile a cry came from Rabbi Getz' wife: "They are killing my husband!" At that moment the police appeared from where they were [apparently] hidden on the Temple Mount. The radio had reported that three Arabs had been killed and many wounded [in the riot], but it was a lie. It was simply an excuse for the police to exercise authority over us and to close down our dig. The police arrested the boys from our Yeshiva and put them in prison. They did nothing to the Arabs. Then they gave orders to immediately erect a new wall [over the entrance to the tunnel] and to close the chambers to prevent any [Jewish] access. [As a result] we lost all connection with the chamber which we were digging [that led to the Ark].[11]

Despite the closure of the site, the rabbis maintained (until the day they died) that they believed they knew exactly where the Ark is located. They never revealed the Ark's precise location for fear the Muslims or others might try to steal or destroy the Ark.

Yet Rabbi Getz admitted that the Israeli government also knows the hiding place of the Ark, but he conceded he believed it would never act on this information for the same reason it will not act on any affair related to the Temple Mount. The political situation is too volatile. Archaeologist Dan Bahat has explained the situation further:

> Why don't we penetrate [the sealed gate] and go in? It is not merely a problem of politics or because behind this wall exists a modern Moslem cistern. This is not the problem. The problem here is that many of the people who are so ardent in keeping the purity of the Temple Mount are afraid that if they trespass the [religious boundary] line...they may come to places which they are not supposed to [enter]. [This is] because these places are too holy, and since we are [ceremonially] impure, it is impossible for them to go inside. This is the reason why observant Jews do not go up to the Temple [Mount]. Unfortunately the Muslims [mis]understood this [as saying] that we don't have any interest in the Temple Mount.[12]

According to Dan Bahat, a further reason for not unsealing the gate is that it would represent a violation of the negotiated limits of Israel's control with the Muslim authorities: "This [Warren's Gate in the Western Wall] is the outer limits of our [Israel's] possession. The [boundary of the] Temple Mount was decided by the early government following the Six-Day War in 1967 and is held by the Muslim authorities to this very day."

The rabbis also stated that they believed that a premature disclosure of the location of the Ark could delay the fulfillment of prophetic events. In this regard, Rabbi Goren once made this comment to writer Louis Rapoport: "The secret will be revealed just prior to building the Third Temple."[11] In like manner, Rabbi Getz once told me of one encounter he had with Lubavitcher rabbis. They said to him: "What will you do with it [the Ark] if you find it? Will you bring tourists to look at it? You better leave it closed until its time will come!"[13]

An Evaluation of the Story

Confirmation of the rabbis' claims is presently impossible since the Wakf and the Israeli government sealed up the Warren's Gate entrance. However, Rabbi Getz' synagogue, built directly on the wall above the sealed entrance to Warren's Gate, continues to be used and bears testimony to the discovery of the ancient gate. When we evaluate the testimony of these witnesses, we should remember that these are leading political and religious figures in Israel, and they have nothing to gain by being discredited by a false rumor of this magnitude. Neither can we doubt that as trained rabbis they know what they have seen. Some rabbis in Israel, most notably Rabbi Nachman Kahane of the Institute for Talmudic Commentaries, doubted that these rabbis actually knew the true location of the Ark. But others, such as Rabbis Israel Ariel and Chaim Richman of the Temple Institute, are convinced their story is accurate.

Therefore, for the time being, the Ark may remain locked in secret behind an entrance blocked with three meters of concrete and steel. In addition, the Antiquities Authority in agreement with the Ministry of Religious Affairs, which oversees the site, has added a stonework facade to the sealed entrance, giving it the appearance that it was never opened! Today, although a small sign identifies Warren's Gate as one of the entrance gates to the Temple Mount, only informed tour guides mention its possible connection with the hiding place of the Ark. However, the Temple Institute in the Jewish Quarter, located a few hundred yards away, assures visitors that the Ark is still safely under the Temple Mount and will be brought out in the near future.

Having heard so many competing theories about the location or discovery of the Ark, what can we really believe? Come with me into the next chapter as we continue our evaluation of eyewitness accounts concerning the search for the Ark.

Entrance to Warren's Gate, sealed with three meters of concrete and steel by the Wakf and the Israeli government.

PART 4

Searching for the Truth About the Ark

11
What Can I Believe?

Now faith is the assurance of things hoped for,
the conviction of things not seen.

—HEBREWS 11:1

The enigmatic Ark of the Covenant has spawned a legion of treasure hunters, each eager to unravel its mysteries and find its secret hiding place. In addition, a multitude of stories, rumors, and claims circulate among the public. Every year new "evidence" for the existence of the Ark emerges, some through the educational and entertainment channels, some through books and newspaper accounts, and others through presentations in churches and conferences. Some people who are involved in this search for the Ark are sincere researchers who are attempting to understand the mystery of the Ark's disappearance, while others are sensationalists seeking only to promote the latest theory. In light of this onslaught of competing theories and allegations, what can we believe? Let us look at some of the reporters' statements about the Ark and judge for ourselves.[1]

Did the Egyptian Pharaoh Neco Have the Ark?

Koinonia House founder and popular Bible teacher and author Chuck Missler has proposed that the Egyptians took the Ark when pharaoh Shishak sacked Jerusalem and plundered the treasures of the Temple (about 926 B.C.) and that the Ethiopians acquired it when the Ethiopian Dynasty (the Twenty-Fifth Dynasty) took control of Egypt (about 730 B.C.). He argues from the biblical account in 2 Chronicles 35:20-25 that when pharaoh Neco II (whom he believes was the last pharaoh of the Ethiopian Dynasty) passed through Israel on his way to aid the Assyrians in their battle at Carchemish, he was carrying the Ark with him. The reason the Judean king Josiah went out to engage him at Megiddo was in order to recover the Ark for Israel. Missler points to Neco's warning to Josiah in 2 Chronicles 35:21: "Stop for your own sake from interfering with God who is with me, so that He will not destroy you," and especially the chronicler's statement: "Josiah...[did not] listen to the words of Neco *from the mouth of God*." Missler finds here a biblical witness to the Ark moving from Egypt to Ethiopia and for Neco possessing the Ark with God's presence attending the Ark and directing Neco.

Missler's novel approach does offer an answer as to how (apart from the Solomon-Sheba myth of the *Kebra Negast*) the Ark came into Ethiopia and why Josiah inexplicably went out to engage Neco without cause and against divine counsel. However, these views present a number of problems. First, Shishak's attack was on Jeroboam's royal palace and the Temple complex. He plundered the Temple treasuries (1 Kings 14:26), which contained the wealth collected by King David for the Temple's maintenance and the utensils for the Temple service (1 Kings 7:51). He also plundered the king's house, which contained 200 shields of gold made by Solomon (1 Kings 10:16). However, the texts do not say Shishak gained entrance to the Temple itself, where the Ark was housed in the Holy of Holies. In fact, we find no evidence for believing that Shishak, or any others who later attacked Jerusalem and took away the treasures of the Temple, took the Ark. For example, in 826 B.C., Jehoash (Joash), King of Israel, plundered the Temple and removed the Temple treasury to Samaria (2 Kings 14:13-14). In 720 B.C., King Ahaz closed the Temple and also emptied its treasury, breaking up Temple furnishings and vessels to pay tribute to the Assyrian king Tiglath-pileser. He also defiled the Temple with a pagan Syrian altar (2 Kings 16:8-18; 2 Chronicles 28:21,24). Likewise, in 695–642 B.C., King Manasseh of Judah placed idols within the Temple, including the Holy Place and the Holy of Holies (2 Kings 21:4-7). Yet the biblical text never states that the Ark was taken in any of these invasions. The only foreign invaders who succeeded in overtaking the Temple were the Babylonians, yet neither biblical nor extrabiblical sources confirm that they took the Ark.

This view also has historical difficulties with its claim that Neco II was part of the Twenty-Fifth (Ethiopian) Dynasty. Neco II (610–595 B.C.) was the son and successor of Psammetichus I (664–610 B.C.), who ended Kushite (Ethiopian) rule and founded the Twenty-Sixth (Saite) Dynasty. Psammetichus I may have ruled for a short time concurrently with Tanutamun (664–656 B.C.), the last Ethiopian pharaoh (the nephew of Taharka, the Ethiopian ruler of the Twenty-Fifth Dynasty),[2] but his rule was in the Delta until he could wrest Upper Egypt from the Ethiopian dynasts. Neco II's relatives clearly did not have any ties with the Ethiopian rulers. Tanutamun in fact killed Neco I (the father of Psammetichus I and the grandfather of Neco II), and Psammetichus I died on the battlefield opposing the Ethiopians (Kushites).[3] Neco II dispatched a military force into Ethiopia[4] as did his son and successor Psammetichus II (595–589 B.C.), whose policy against the Ethiopians was so fierce that he erased from the monuments in Egypt the names of the Ethiopian rulers of the Twenty-Fifth Dynasty.[5] Moreover, Thutmose III had established the cult of Amun in Nubia, and the Kushite (Ethiopian) priests of Amun developed into the Twenty-Fifth (Ethiopian) Dynasty. So by the time they took on the accoutrements of pharaonic power, they had already adopted the cult of Amun based in their homeland.[6] Therefore, even if they had come into possession of the Ark, as the symbol of a foreign religion it would have meant nothing to them and might even have been destroyed by them as a rival cult object.

Josiah's untimely death, recorded with the most detail in 2 Chronicles 35, has another reasonable historical explanation. The Assyrian and Babylonian chronicles and the ostracon of Hashavyahu help us understand why Josiah went to war with pharaoh Neco. These documents affirm that the kingdom of Judah had expanded to the west and that Neco was allied with the Assyrians against the Babylonians, who had overrun the southern part of Assyria and pushed the Assyrians back from Haran. At this time, Josiah was either an ally of the Babylonians or at least an enemy of the Assyrians, and he saw Neco's aid to the Assyrians as a threat to his newly gained freedom from Assyrian hegemony and territorial expansion.[7]

But what about the warning from God, who was with the Egyptians (2 Chronicles 35:21), not to go to war? The references to the pharaoh's deity probably point to an Egyptian god taken into battle with him (probably in statuary form). We can translate all the references in verse 21 as "god," and the "words" in verse 22 as "from the mouth of an idol." This is the way many writers of the Talmud and the Aramaic Targum understood it, justifying Josiah's rejection of the words as the empty threat of a pagan. Yet the words of warning, according to the Hebrew chronicler, seem to be "from the mouth of God" and seem to imply that Josiah was disobedient in rejecting them. This is the way the Jewish apocryphal work 1 Esdras saw it, making the message to Josiah come from the prophet Jeremiah (mentioned in verse 25) and taking all the references to deity in verse 21 to be the one true God (1 Esdras 1:26-27). In the rabbinic commentary Leviticus Rabba (to Leviticus 1:18), we read that Jeremiah understood God to be working out His own program through the actions of Neco (regardless of Neco's intent) and so interpreted the pharaoh's warning as a word from the Lord. Because Josiah decided against the prophet's advice and opposed Neco, the Lord allowed him to be killed. Even if Jeremiah was not involved, Josiah should have heeded Neco's words from his god because they were indirectly a warning from Josiah's God. How would Josiah have known this? According to the rabbinic work *Ta'anit* (22b), God punished Josiah because he should have consulted the prophet before going out to battle and did not do so. The implication is that had he done so, he would have understood God's warning through Neco, but failing to do so was an act of disobedience worthy of death. This is probably the best way to understand this difficult text.[8]

The remaining problem is that the same text (2 Chronicles 35) which Missler uses for his argument that Neco had the Ark may in fact teach the opposite: The Ark may still have been in Israel's possession in the time of Josiah, and he rather than Neco may have had the Ark and returned it to the Temple. Second Chronicles 35:3 records the king's command to the Levites: "Put (or leave) the holy ark in the house which Solomon the son of David king of Israel built; it will be a burden on your shoulders no longer. Now serve the LORD your God and His people Israel." This has been taken either as a description of the historic function of the Levites, that is, that the Levites used to carry the Ark before it was put in the Temple now only serve Israel, or as a present injunction to stop carrying around the Ark and to reinstall it in the newly dedicated Temple. Alternately, many rabbis understood it to mean, "Take the Ark, which you have been carrying to keep it safe, and leave it in the Temple's hidden chamber where it will remain safe." I have already dealt with the interpretation of this passage in chapter 9, but here am concerned with Missler's interpretation that though this was a present command by King Josiah to the Levites, they were unable to fulfill it because they did not have the Ark. The chronicler tends to explain theological difficulties, so if this was a command that was not obeyed, we can be sure it would have received comment. One need only compare the simple statement of Josiah's death in 2 Kings with the detailed explanation in 2 Chronicles to understand this point. However, the response to Josiah's commands (2 Chronicles 35:3-6) is given in verse 10: "So the service was prepared, and the priests stood at their stations and the Levites by their divisions *according to the king's command.*" If verse 3 is taken as a command to the Levites, verse 10 affirms that they obeyed that command.

Therefore, we find no basis in history or in the biblical text that the Egyptians had the Ark, that it transferred to Ethiopian control during the Twenty-Fifth Dynasty, or that it played any role in the account of Josiah's death in 2 Chronicles 35.

Did the Ethiopian Eunuch Know About the Ark?

Cornuke and Halbrook, as well as Missler, believe that the Ethiopian eunuch mentioned in Acts 8:27, who was a court official of Candace, queen of the Ethiopians, and in charge of all her treasure, came to Jerusalem seeking to return the Ark to the Messiah, whose deeds had been reported in their land. We should first note, however, that the Ethiopia of the first century was not the modern-day Ethiopia (Abyssinia) but rather the region of ancient

Nubia. Second, the text in Acts states that the Ethiopian eunuch came to Jerusalem for personal worship (which Gentile converts did at the Feast of Pentecost) and not on official business. He apparently was not looking for the Messiah, for only when he was leaving was he approached by Philip and told about Jesus (Acts 8:28-34). So why would these authors argue that his journey had something to do with the Ark in Ethiopia?

In Ethiopian tradition, Queen Candace is the Christian ruler of Axum, the repository of the Ark, and is merged with the tradition about the queen of Sheba. One of the foremost authorities on Ethiopia has observed: "Ethiopians are not conscious of any dichotomy here, for the complete blending of Jewish and Christian traditions into one indissoluble whole is one of the most remarkable features of the syncretistic Abyssinian civilization."[9] This confusion of the queen of Sheba legend with the New Testament account of Candace probably resulted from the similarity of the stories being circulated by the Ethiopians about Solomon and Sheba and about Alexander and Candace. At some point they were blended together and became one tradition (even though separated by hundreds of years). In fact, Candace became the hereditary title of Ethiopian queens. Authors who are uncritical of Ethiopian traditions such as this may misinterpret passages with references to (or imagined references to) Ethiopia, especially where the text is lacking sufficient explanation of an event, such as with the Ethiopian eunuch. As tantalizing as such an interpretation may seem, it has no biblical or historical support. The account may have been included in the New Testament simply to demonstrate the Gentiles' inclusion in the church and to show the geographical extent of the gospel at this early period.

Was the Ark Secretly Moved to Jerusalem?

Canadian author Grant Jeffrey, who holds the Ethiopian theory, has told a story for more than a decade that the Ark was removed from the Saint Mary Church of Zion in Axum and secretly transported to Israel. According to Jeffrey a "rescue mission" took place in 1991 at the close of the Ethiopian civil war. Israeli Mossad agents supposedly paid $42 million to Ethiopian generals to allow Israeli elite special forces to take the Ark to a "secure and secret repository" near Jerusalem where it waits today for the rebuilding of the Third Temple. Jeffrey cites as sources a late Canadian diplomat (who was a friend of his family) and unnamed rabbis in Israel. He also once told me that he had a source in the Israeli military corroborate the story. While Jeffrey may need to protect his sources, the only way his story can be independently checked is for all of his sources to be made public.

I mentioned this story to the late rabbis Shlomo Goren and Meir Yehuda Getz, the official rabbis with the most direct access to such knowledge in Israel at the time. Both said that they had never heard such a story and reaffirmed their contention that the Ethiopian location was impossible because the Ark could have never been taken as the *Kebra Negast* records. This was Rabbi Goren's response:

> It is a joke!...The ten tribes didn't even take the Ark with them when they were exiled from Israel because they didn't govern [control] the place of the Ark. They were in Samaria and the Ark was in Jerusalem, so they couldn't get to it. So how could the Ethiopians?[10]

Rabbi Getz on several occasions told me that anyone, including a rabbi, who said he or she had the Ark, was mistaken.

The Ark, he maintained, still existed beneath the Temple Mount and would be brought out in the future when the time was ready.

I also asked one of the Ethiopian priests (in Israel), who said he had government connections and was in a place to know, if he had ever heard of the Ark being moved from Axum to Jerusalem. He was upset by the suggestion and stated that it would be impossible for anyone to get the Ark since it is highly guarded by Christian monks. Moreover, the Ethiopian Orthodox Church accepts the teaching of the *Kebra Negast* that the Jews have been disinherited by God and that Ethiopia is the new Israel. They would therefore have no reason to negotiate with Jews or the State of Israel over the Ark, by which their rulers alone maintain the right to rule and through which Ethiopia has attained its national destiny. And, of course, the Ethiopians still maintain the Ark and is with them today (not in Israel).

Has Anyone Seen the Ark?

A number of eyewitnesses claim to have seen the Ark—under the Temple Mount, under Gordon's Calvary, under Mount Nebo, and in the Chapel of the Tablet in Ethiopia. Obviously, if there is only one true Ark, it cannot exist simultaneously in multiple places! Conversely, this does leave open the possibility that one of these sightings is true. Let us consider some of the stories connected with the leading theories of the Ark's location and decide for ourselves whether anyone has seen the Ark.

Did Someone See the Ark in Ethiopia?

Authors Bob Cornuke and David Halbrook have reported in 2002 the eyewitness account of a monk named Haile Sclassic ("Might of the Trinity"), the curator of the Axum Museum in Ethiopia. Although supposedly allowed access to the Saint Mary of Zion Church by the government in order to catalog its treasures, Mr. Selassie had used subterfuge to gain an unscheduled entrance to the Chapel of the Tablet to view the Ark at the instigation of the authors. He said he was escorted to the inner sanctuary where the sacred object was housed and found it was inside "a silver box" within "a stone vault." Once a monk had opened the doors of the box that contained the Ark, immediately a golden reflection off the Ark rendered Mr. Selassie and the two monks that accompanied him unconscious. They were taken to a hospital where later the two monks died and Mr. Selassie reported his vision had been affected. In spite of his ordeal he was able to describe the Ark as "a wooden box, covered with gold," with a golden top containing two "chest high figurines" with "feathery arms overshadowing the mercy seat, spread out" to make a seat "where someone might sit."[11]

Some aspects of this account apparently concerned Cornuke and Halbrook, despite their urge to accept the story they had waited a year to hear.

> Had they actually seen the genuine ark? Or had the thought of the ark's awesome power, magnified by a lifetime of potent religious indoctrination, overwhelmed their guilty consciences? Perhaps the idea of the ark's holy and unapproachable stature struck such fear in their hearts that they fell back, as if slain, at the first glint of a metallic reflection.... Whatever they saw—a tangible object or a hallucination—it had inflicted a devastating toll."[12]

However, before we jump to a conclusion based on the previous testimony, let us hear another eyewitness who claims to also have had access to the Axum "Ark" and has lived to tell about it. Although not a "government official" like Cornuke's Mr. Selassie, this witness has sufficient credentials to be heard. He is Professor Edward Ullendorff, the first incumbent of the only Chair of Ethiopian Studies in Great Britain. His book *Ethiopia and the Bible,* published by Oxford University Press, is acknowledged as the classic scholarly work in the field on religion in Ethiopia. When Graham Hancock's book on the Ark in Ethiopia, *The Sign and the Seal,* was first released, the press sought Ullendorff as an expert to give his evaluation of Hancock's theory. In an interview with the *Los Angeles Times*, Ullendorff, after calling Hancock's book "a sad joke," declared that he had personally seen the object in Axum: "They have a wooden box, but it's empty.... Middle to late medieval construction, when these were fabricated *ad hoc.*"[13] Ullendorff went on to say that the priests and the government perpetuate an aura of mystery around the object "mostly to maintain the idea that it's a venerated object." Yet Hancock and Cornuke, as well as other Westerners who have visited the site, have claimed that no one is permitted to enter the church and view the Ark.

Ullendorf, to the contrary, says this is simply because they were Westerners who had no knowledge of Ethiopian language or customs: "I've seen it. There was no problem getting access when I saw it in 1941.... You need to be able to speak their language, classical Ge'ez; you need to be able to show that you're serious."[14] Therefore, according to this expert witness, the object in Axum is a medieval relic that can be viewed by anyone whom the priests choose to let see it.

Because the *Kebra Negast* supports the claim of the royal house, it has become the national epic of the country and the possession of its "ark" is essential to maintaining Abyssian Christian supercession. It is also held to be the Ark by the "faithful" and generally acknowledged as such by the entire population, who regard it as part of their national pride. Therefore, regardless of what is in the Axum chapel, Ethiopians still claim it is the Ark.

Did Someone See the Ark in Jerusalem?

The late Ron Wyatt was among one of the first who claimed to have seen—and discovered—the Ark of the Covenant in Jerusalem. This is from an account of his alleged discovery under the escarpment of Mount Calvary, which he believed to be "Jeremiah's Grotto":

> On Wednesday, January 6, 1982, Ron discovered the cave chamber where the Ark and other temple items had been hidden over 2600 years before. The chamber was about 22 feet by 12 feet, although not exactly rectangular as one corner narrowed in. The chamber was filled almost to the ceiling with rocks. Beneath the rocks were dry-rotted timbers and dry-rotted animal skins, apparently undisturbed for quite some time. Beneath the rocks, timbers and animal skins were missing items from the first temple, including the Table of Shewbread. At the far end of the chamber was a stone case, and housed within the stone case was the Ark of the Covenant, complete and intact, except that the carrying staves had been removed. Ron was the first human to set eyes on these priceless items since they had been secreted from the city prior to its destruction in 586 B.C.[15]

This most novel of sites has been proposed as the hiding place of the Ark because Wyatt imagines it fits the concept of Jesus as the High Priest offering the final blood atonement. Wyatt speculated that Jesus was crucified against the side of this hill and that His blood must have run through a socket hole at the base of the cross and then dripped down through a crack in the mountain (caused by the earthquake recorded in Matthew 27:51), finally landing on the mercy seat of the Ark, positioned on the exact spot in a subterranean chamber some 60 feet beneath the mountain.[16] Wyatt says that God had arranged for the Ark to be hidden in this chamber 600 years before Christ died in order to give mankind one final warning before the seven plagues of Revelation consume the earth.

Wyatt sells a videotape of his various adventures, which includes a segment showing him squeezing through an opening within a cavern inside Gordon's Calvary. His video documentary of this event, narrated by his wife, gives the following account of the discovery:

> In January of 1982, after steadily digging in a cave system since 1979, he busted through the rock into a chamber, which contained a gold table and several other artifacts, which Ron believed to be from the First Temple. Then, farther back, he saw the top of a stone case, which appeared to be the correct size to contain the Ark of the Covenant. Overwhelmed with emotion and double pneumonia, Ron passed out in that chamber for 45 minutes. He knew what was in that case, but now what? He attempted to photograph it with a Polaroid camera, a 35mm camera, and video. In every case, the photos were a whiteout. He returned home to recover and work until he could afford to return. In May, he borrowed a colonoscope and went back. Drilling a small hole through the case, he was able to see enough to positively identify the contents of the stone case—it was the Ark![17]

Wyatt claimed to have taken and tested a blood sample from the Ark and declared it to be Christ's blood! Despite the magnitude of such a discovery, nothing was ever removed from the supposed chamber, except, as Wyatt claims, an ivory pomegranate (later sold by Wyatt to the Israel Museum). Therefore, there has never been any evidence of the alleged finds. According to Australian Jonathan Gray, an "international explorer, biblical archaeologist and lecturer": "Everything's still there [in the cave], just where Ron found it, completely hidden and very well guarded."[18] Wyatt had claimed an angel told him to leave the items in the cave. According to Gray, the site is being guarded by the Israeli government, who has banned anyone from reentering the cave system. Nevertheless, Gray was confident that they would soon make the discovery public. At the time this statement was made, Wyatt was still alive, and Gray wrote of his intention to reenter the cave with the Israeli authorities and a film crew, showing them the Ark and, with a team of genetic scientists, taking and testing another sample of blood from the Ark.

Since Wyatt's death in 1999, his widow, Mary Nell, and Richard Rives, president of Wyatt Archaeological Research, have continued to promote Wyatt's claim and financed a 2003 excavation within the Second Temple period quarry known popularly as "Solomon's Quarries" and "Zedekiah's Cave" (based on the traditional belief that the escape route of the king reported in 2 Kings 25:4 is located at this site). Their belief, based solely on Wyatt's conjecture, is that a passageway exists between the chamber of the Temple treasures and their site near the Damascus Gate.[19] They believe at the end of the passageway, should they discover it, lies the Ark of the Covenant.

Evaluating Wyatt's Claim

The bottom line in evaluating Wyatt's claim is that he has never produced a single shred of verifiable evidence to validate it.

The general rule in such matters is this: The greater the claim, the greater the evidence needed to support it. However, he has produced not one photograph or collaborating eyewitness to such an incredible discovery—even after two decades and after Wyatt and his associates have produced several books and films.

Wyatt was a Seventh-day Adventist, and the sensational nature of his claims, which lacked evidence to support them, brought discredit to his denomination and led church authorities to investigate and publish their findings. The first to do so was the Horn Archaeological Museum connected with Andrews University, an official Seventh-day Adventist institution. They released a packet of documents, including correspondence with Wyatt, that denounced his claims and warned the public against accepting his unfounded statements.[20] Next followed a book by popular Seventh-day Adventist pastors and authors Russell and Colin Standish, *Holy Relics or Revelation: Recent Astounding Archaeological Claims Evaluated*. Russell Standish holds a Ph.D. from the University of Sydney in Psychology and Colin Standish is an Internist (consultant physician). They spent hundreds of hours researching each of Wyatt's claims and interviewing his contacts as well as his associates. They wrote this regarding their concerns in publishing their evaluation:

> We write with a great burden for the souls of God's flock and its unity in Christian love and truth. We have set as our task, the thorough documentation of the numerous defects and deficiencies in Ron Wyatt's claims. God's people deserve no less. There are enough unsubstantiated claims, erroneous assertions, denigration of those who have shown Ron's claims to be faulty, and resort to guesswork in the Wyatt and Gray

> books and presentations, to arouse the deep concerns of Christians of all faiths.[21]

With respect to their investigation of Wyatt's eyewitness account of the Ark, especially after comparing it with the biblical description, they made this conclusion:

> Because of these significant discrepancies [from the biblical description] we are compelled to reject Ron Wyatt's ark as being that which once graced both the tabernacle and the Temple of Solomon. If Ron Wyatt has seen an ark as he has described, then it was a bogus imitation of the genuine. In view of these facts it would be a worthless pursuit to attempt to put forward yet further alibis to provide a platform for Ron Wyatt's faulty claim. Remember no one, no one, has ever viewed the Wyatt Ark of the Covenant. Why would any sincere individual desire to conjure up further implausible theories to sustain an "archaeological find" which has never been verified?[22]

Wyatt claimed to have found, touched, and even scraped blood off the Ark, as well as handled the tablets of the Ten Commandments inside the Ark. The Bible warned that none but the special order of priests known as the Kohathites were to handle the Ark. Indeed, an improper handling of the Ark by Uzzah had resulted in death. Yet, although Ron Wyatt was unharmed, he declared that numbers of others who tried to enter the chamber since had died in the attempt! This arrogance underlies the sensationalism of Wyatt's claims and cautions anyone who might be inclined to believe them—in spite of the absence of any evidence two decades after his self-styled discovery of more than

90 artifacts of biblical significance—that the only basis for belief is the testimony (and character) of Wyatt himself.

From an archaeological evaluation, the site of Wyatt's "Calvary" is part of a tomb complex reliably dated to the First Temple period. While this might conceivably fit the time period for the hiding of the Ark in "Jeremiah's Grotto," it would disqualify it as the place for the crucifixion of Jesus (which took place at the end of the Second Temple period)—a fact required by Wyatt since his argument rests on the Ark's hiding place being associated with this event.[23] Early Church history, Roman pagan accounts, and modern archaeological excavation together make a strong case for the Church of the Holy Sepulcher, not the Garden Tomb, being the historical site for the death, burial, and resurrection of Jesus.[24] We have seen that Wyatt's interpretation of physical evidences at his site in relation to the crucifixion was more fiction than fact. Without any documentation of his astounding claims, his detailed description of his excavation discoveries amounts to nothing more than an imaginative story.

A religious evaluation would also disqualify this site because as a tomb complex it was a place of Jewish ceremonial impurity. Since the Temple priests hid the Ark to protect its sanctity from defilement by the Babylonians, they would never deliberately choose a place of defilement. Moreover, Wyatt says that God chose this execution spot for Jesus' crucifixion so that His blood could fall through a crack in the hill and land directly on the mercy seat of the Ark, fulfilling its typological meaning. However, nowhere in the Old Testament is such a typological relationship implied between the Ark and Christ. The New Testament book of Hebrews makes a statement associating Christ's blood with the Holy Place, but it specifically refers to "heavenly things" and not "the copies of the things in the heavens," such as the Ark

(Hebrews 9:23). In fact, the theological contrast being made by the author of Hebrews in this section, in which the spiritual application of Christ's blood ("a better sacrifice") is reserved for heaven (Hebrews 9:24), contradicts Wyatt's literal notion that Christ's shed blood needed to fall on the earthly Ark. However, Wyatt's view does advance the unbiblical position of replacement theology that teaches that Israel was replaced by the church as the people of God and therefore no longer has any promise of national blessing. Correspondence with me by Jim Pinkowsky, one of Wyatt's associates, affirmed this as one of Wyatt's tenets. Obviously, this perspective, rather than biblical teaching, governed Wyatt's fabrication of his story.

Other Reported Sightings of the Ark in Jerusalem

Another reported eyewitness account of the Ark in Jerusalem was allegedly made by Rabbi Matiyahu (Mati) Dan Hacohen, founder of the Ateret Cohanim Yeshiva, who was one of those helping rabbis Goren and Getz secretly excavate from within the Warren's Gate underneath the Temple Mount in search of the chamber of the Ark. Dr. David Lewis, author and founder of Christians United for Israel, has written that Hacohen disclosed to him the following account, which was allegedly tape recorded (although the tape has never since been found):[25]

> Hacohen told of how they were excavating along the lower level of the Western Wall of the Temple Mountain. At one point during the night, they came to a doorway in the Western Wall. Passing through this doorway, the crew entered a fairly long tunnel. At the end of the tunnel, Rabbi Hacohen said: "I saw the golden ark that once stood in the Holy Place of the

> Temple of the Almighty." It was covered with old, dried animal skins of some kind. However one gold, gleaming end of the ark was visible. He could see the loops or rounds of gold through which the poles of acacia wood could be thrust so that the ark could be properly carried by four dedicated Levites. Hacohen and his friends rushed out to the home of Chief Rabbi Shlomo Goren. They awakened the rabbi and excitedly told him that they had discovered the holy ark of the covenant! Goren said, "We are ready for this event. We have already prepared the poles of acacia wood and have Levites who can be standing by in the morning to carry out the ark in triumph." [26]

I asked Rabbi Goren about the factual nature of this account, since Hacohen worked with him and supposedly reported the sighting to him. His response was nothing short of emphatic. "They are all liars! They are just telling you stories! How can anyone say they saw the Ark? The Ark is hundreds of meters down.... If [anyone] would see the Ark he wouldn't remain alive even for one minute!"

Today, Rabbi Hacohen denies that he ever told such a story, or he claims that what he said was totally misunderstood. Hacohen's present position, and that of his Yeshiva Ateret Cohanim, is that the Temple Mount is off limits to Jews according to rabbinic injunction because of the Ark's presence beneath the site. If he held this same conviction in 1981, he would not have been likely to enter the holiest of all holy places and gaze upon the holiest of all objects.

Another story of the Ark being seen during the Warren's Gate excavation has been attributed to Rabbi Getz himself. I first heard this story from Jimmy DeYoung, who had interviewed Rabbi

Getz as part our collaboration on his video and my book (with Thomas Ice) entitled *Ready to Rebuild.* According to Jimmy, the comment, though recorded, was made "off the record" at Getz' request. According to Jimmy, Rabbi Getz claimed that when the chamber leading to the Ark was discovered, he was afraid to go in and look upon the Ark. So using a mirror, he looked around a corner of the tunnel and beheld the reflected image of the Ark.

In order to confirm this story from the source, I interviewed Rabbi Getz on film in his office. I took along Rabbi Chaim Richman, who had also heard the story and also wanted to get clarification. When I repeated the story to Rabbi Getz, he was surprised to hear that such a story was circulating about him. Wanting to set the record straight he said: "No, no that is not what I said. These are all stories....I am not responsible for someone else's remarks. It is important to know the truth since millions of Christians and people who love Israel read such material."[27]

Rabbis Goren and Getz made it quite clear that they never reached the chamber of the Ark. They stated that by their calculations they were at least a year and a half away from reaching it. Rabbi Goren was also enraged to think that anyone would think they could view the Ark by whatever means. He had told me that he had no intention of removing the Ark if they reached it. Moreover, I interviewed two others who had been involved with Goren and Getz in the tunnel—Gershon Salomon, founder of the Temple Mount Faithful organization, and his associate Zev Bar-Tov. Both stated on camera that they had never heard either rabbi—or anyone else in the secret group of excavators—say that the Ark had been found or seen.

In seeking to understand how this story came about—or how Rabbi Getz' words were "misunderstood," I offer the following. Rabbi Getz (who understood English and spoke it fairly well) preferred to conduct his interviews only in Hebrew. At his interview, Jimmy DeYoung, who is not fluent in Hebrew, relied upon his translator, who was also pastor at his church, to understand Rabbi Getz. When I asked the translator if he heard Getz make this statement he replied that he had not. So, somewhere, something was lost—or in this case gained—in translation. This story continues to circulate in Christian groups, and for this reason I have cited here the negations of those directly involved.

By evaluating these various eyewitness accounts, we can see conflicts in the details of the description of the Ark. The rabbis' own reports of the extent of their clandestine excavations within Warren's Gate do not support the other accounts. Let us weigh these statements in light of these facts and testimony.

The Problem of the Ark's Location

The primary problem with these stories is that they claim that the excavators reached the site of the Ark itself. According to Rabbi Getz, their excavation reached within some 96 feet of the Holy of Holies, calculated apparently from the wall they estimated was 9 to 12 feet from the western section of the warning wall, which, according to rabbinic sources, was located only 15 feet from the Holy of Holies. In addition, Rabbi Goren contends that the chamber that houses the Ark is located deeper still beneath the Holy of Holies: "I believe that the Ark is there, but we must dig not a few meters, but hundreds of meters to reach it." He estimated that an excavation from the farthest point to which they penetrated to this chamber would take at least a year and a half.

Despite these statements, I again pressed Rabbi Getz as to whether he had actually been in this room where the Ark was stored. His reply was in agreement with that of Rabbi Goren:

> We know where it is, but we did not discover it. According to the [rabbinic] writings [the place] is called the *Gear Ha'Etzem* ("the Chalk of the Bone") and is located deep within the ground. I wanted to go through the tunnels [and reach this area], since I knew the direction—I might only be off only 15–18 feet—but it is impossible [to reach] because it is deep under the water [which flooded the tunnels].[28]

If we take these rabbis, who directed the excavation, at their word, then there is no possible way that they could have come even to the place of the Ark, much less seen it. The additional matter remains as to whether or not they *would* have looked at it if they could have reached it. On the one hand, many Christians believe that when the Shekinah was absent from the Ark it was simply a harmless relic. After all, Bezalel and Oholiab had touched the Ark while constructing it. On the other hand, these rabbis also believe that the Shekinah never left Jerusalem, and the tractate *Shekalim* in the Mishnah records the instant death of a priest who so much as sought to reveal the location of the Ark. Based on this belief, Rabbi Goren categorically denied that Rabbi Hacohen or Rabbi Getz or anyone else could ever see the Ark. What then, are we to make of these reports? Gershon Salomon, Director of the Temple Mount Faithful, when asked whether he had heard the rabbis or anyone else say they had seen the Ark, replied: "I did not hear anyone say that they found it. What I heard is what Rabbi Getz said very clearly in those days: 'We are at an important point in history. After 2500 years we are marching to the place of the Ark of the Covenant, and we must do it quickly!' He was wonderful, and he was determined to do it!"

What Should We Believe?

What can we believe with respect to claims about the Ark? To the degree that a claim offers substantial evidence, we have grounds for belief, but the less it offers, the less we are obligated to believe. Put simply, until we have more tangible proof for the location of the Ark, we have only researched theories, sincere opinions, and even visionary experiences. But is this sufficient to warrant our hoping for a day when the Ark will finally be revealed? In our final chapter we will consider this as we seek to answer the question, Will the Ark ever be discovered?"

12
Will the Ark Ever Be Discovered?

When the Holy One, blessed be He, in His mercy will again build His Temple and His Holy Place, He will restore them [the Ark, the menorah, the heavenly fire, and the Urim and Thummim] to their position in order to gladden Jerusalem.

—NUMBERS RABBAH 15:10

Many people today contend that the Ark will never be discovered. Their arguments often go beyond those that we considered in chapter 5, which dealt with its historical disappearance. The concern of these objectors is not that it has been lost and might one day be recovered, but that it vanished and should never reappear because it has already performed its purpose on earth. Jews who hold this view apply it to the whole of the ceremonial system. The Temple and its sacrifices are not necessary for the Jewish people today. This primitive ritual of the past is gone, and a more enlightened Jewry has moved beyond such things to the spiritual realities they were meant to convey. For many Christians who hold this view, the Ark symbolized the presence of God, which Christ fulfilled at the Incarnation. He is the new Ark of God, and therefore no other Ark is needed, nor should we seek for it.

Replacement Theology and the Ark

Some Christian denominations who hold to replacement theology (a view that the church has superseded and therefore replaced Israel as the people of God) teach that the Ark, like every shadow-symbol of the Tabernacle and Temple, had to pass away in order for Christ to be the antitypical fulfillment. This theological position is set in stone (literally) in Israel at a Roman Catholic site in the village of Abu Gosh (ancient Kiriath-jearim), where the Ark once rested in the days of the prophet Samuel. Today, the Sisters of Saint Joseph of the Apparition maintain the Our Lady Ark of the Covenant Church on the top of the hill where tradition locates the house of Abinadab, the priest who tended the Ark. On the top of this church, dedicated in 1924, is a huge stone statue that makes a striking statement. The Ark of the Covenant is present, but standing on top of the Ark between the cherubim is Mary, holding in one of her arms the baby Jesus. In baby Jesus' hands are two objects: the tablets of Moses (the old covenant) and the manna. A publication sold at the church explains the symbolism of this statue:

Our Lady Ark of the Covenant Church in Abu Gosh with Statue of Mary and Jesus on top of the Ark.

During the days of its pilgrimage, the Church looks to Mary, Ark of the New Covenant, as its model.... Mary is also an inspiration for the Church as she, like the Ark, was the repository of God's presence and holiness.... Through Mary, God will become present to us in a new and wondrous way, just as the Cloud is described in Exodus as overshadowing the Tent of Meeting which housed the Ark.... Mary, "overshadowed" by the Most High, became the repository not simply of the tablets of the Law, but of the Law-giver Himself; not simply of the desert manna, but of the Living Bread from heaven. Hence they called her by such titles as Abode of the King, Tabernacle of the Lord, Ark of Holiness, and Ark of the Covenant....as David danced before the Ark, so the child in Elizabeth's womb leapt for joy. And as the Ark was left by David in the house of Abinadab for three months, bringing it a blessing, so Mary brought a blessing to the house of Zachary and Elizabeth where she stayed for three months. Mary is indeed the "Mother of my Lord," an honorific title in the Old Testament by virtue of her being the Ark of the New Covenant.... Likewise, the cherubim bowing down over the Ark and hiding their faces in a posture of awe and adoration before Yahweh...and cry "Holy, Holy, Holy, Lord God of Hosts." In the same way, Mary in her Immaculate Conception stands out as uniquely exemplifying the holiness of God.... She is the Inmost shrine, the Holy of Holies overshadowed by the Cloud of the Holy Spirit and encompassing in her very body the Holy One Himself.[1]

In other words, Mary is the true Ark of the Covenant and a repository for the presence of God—Jesus, the New Covenant. Since both represent the new revelation of God, they replace the old revelation (the original Ark), which as a symbol has now passed away. This interpretation is graphically portrayed by depicting the cherubim on the statue facing outward, rather than inward, as on the original Ark. This symbolizes God's departed glory, which replacement theology teaches will never again return because it has already returned in the person of Christ.

Judaism's Belief in the Return of the Ark

In contrast to Christian replacement theology, the rabbinic Judaism that formed after the destruction of the Second Temple continued to hold to the belief that the Temple vessels, foremost of which is the Ark, would be restored in the end of days with the final restoration of Israel. Rabbi Leibel Reznick states this position:

> Jewish tradition has always maintained that the treasures would remain until the coming of the Messiah. Muslim tradition forbids the site [the Temple Mount] from being explored. Curiosity is nature's most powerful force. Tradition is God's immovable object of faith. Here on the Temple Mount we find the answer to that ancient conundrum, "What happens when an irresistible force meets an immovable object?" for the treasures are yet to be discovered.[2]

Orthodox Jews connected with the Temple movement in Israel promote this belief, but they are often indifferent in their response to the questions of curious tourists regarding the Ark since they regard them as not having a true spiritual apprehension of the religious issues involved. For example, Rabbi Chaim Richman of the Temple Institute once said in response to a question as to when the Ark would be found: "The Ark of the Covenant is still hidden. There are things that we as humans must do, and there are things that G-d will do for us at the proper time."[3] The rabbi's reply understood one of the teachings of the late Rabbi Kook, who laid the spiritual foundation for Jews such as those in the Temple movement, that the messianic age will not arrive until the Jewish people collectively attain a higher state of spirituality. Then, in response to the Jewish nation, God, like a bridegroom to a bride, will act upon His prophetic promises. Therefore, at the present time, Jewish institutions such as the Temple Institute are faithfully constructing the vessels that will be used in the rebuilt Temple. Along with the inventory of Temple treasures they are making, they display a model of the Ark that one of their craftsman has made to the exact specifications. However, they are careful to tell visitors to their center that they have no intention of constructing another Ark, because they know the location of the original (under the Temple Mount), and they intend to restore it to the new Temple when the proper time arrives. According to the ancient Jewish sources, that day will be when the Third Temple returns to the Temple Mount: "I will cause My Shekinah to dwell in it [the Third Temple] in glory" (Targum *Jonathan on the Prophets* on Haggai 1:8).

Gershon Salomon, Founder and Director of the Temple Mount Faithful, also believes that the Ark will be returned to a new Temple. He says that the return of the Ark may well usher in this long-expected day: "We want to make all mankind again one family of God. We want to make all mankind worshippers of the One God here in Jerusalem on the holy hill, Mount Moriah—the Temple Mount. One of the important things that is connected to this great event is the Ark of the Covenant."[4] Salomon, like Rabbi Richman, respects the proper timing of God's plan, and he argues that the recovery of the Ark would necessitate the rebuilding of the Temple: "The Ark of the Covenant cannot be put in a museum, nor in a synagogue, but in only one place, the Temple. We know that the generation of the destruction of the First Temple hid the Ark of the Covenant for the time of the Third Temple, the last and eternal Temple."[5] Following Jewish tradition and his conviction from his days digging in search of the Ark with rabbis Goren and Getz, Salomon has often written in his newsletter, *Voice of the Temple Mount,* that the Ark will soon be brought out from its hiding place under the Temple Mount and installed in the Third Temple. Salomon believes that the chamber of the Ark is accessed from below the well of the souls, the very place Montique Parker tried so hard to reach. While he does not envision another dig for the Ark being allowed under the present government officials supervising the site, he hopes that through the political efforts of a group such as his, the government will assert sovereignty over the Temple Mount, rebuild the Temple, and recover the Ark.

Ultraorthodox or Hasidic Judaism and mystical or Kabbalistic Judaism also believe that the Ark will be restored from its secret place of hiding, but with a difference. Along with the Ark and every Temple treasure, every stone of the original Temple will also return as well. As the Zohar states, "And all the foundations of the Holy Temple have gone into secret hiding places, none have been lost, not even one. And when the Holy One Blessed be He returns, and restores Jerusalem to her original place, those original stone foundations will return to their places" (*Pekuday,* p. 480). The belief here is that the Temple was inviolate and its sanctity was preserved by the Almighty by removing it to

Himself while allowing only an appearance of destruction to take place. Some contend that the fully constructed Temple will descend from heaven in holy fire to reoccupy its original place on a properly purified Temple Mount.

Where do these modern Jews get the idea of a future restoration of the Ark and the Temple vessels? Although a matter of interpretation, they have evidently drawn their expectation from the Bible and the Jewish traditions based upon it. Let us look at some of these and consider their belief in a fulfillment in the future.

The Fulfillment in the Future

When the Jewish remnant returned from exile to Jerusalem, the first prophetic voice they heard was Haggai's. He gave his message to provoke his people to finish the Second Temple after a lapse in the rebuilding. As he exhorted the people to complete this Temple, which appeared inferior to the First Temple, the prophet gave a prophecy concerning the future of the Temple:

> For thus says the LORD of hosts, "Once more in a little while, I am going to shake the heavens and the earth, the sea also and the dry land. I will shake all the nations; and they will come with the wealth of all nations, and I will fill this house with glory," says the LORD of hosts. "The silver is Mine, and the gold is Mine," declares the LORD of hosts. "The latter glory of this house will be greater than the former," says the LORD of hosts, "and in this place I will give peace," declares the LORD of hosts (Haggai 2:6-9).

Many commentators argue that these words were spoken of the Second Temple to encourage them in its rebuilding. However, in terms of a literal historical fulfillment of this prophecy, the Second Temple must be considered a failure. If we attempt to make the Second Temple fulfill these extensive restoration prophecies, then either we must abandon any sense of literal interpretation (which the details of the text cannot bear) or admit that the Word of God itself has failed (which orthodox theology cannot bear). This has often been done by Christians interpreting the peace brought by Jesus' death on the cross as "the latter glory" of the Temple. However, such an interpretation forces the rest of the prophecy to be reinterpreted in a nonliteral manner to fit with this conclusion. Consequently, Jewish interpreters have not seen the Second Temple in view in this prophecy because, as the Tosefta *(Yom Tov)* explained, its builders realized *it was not yet the time* to build such a Temple since Israel's complete restoration had not yet been attained. In like manner, Rashi, one of the greatest medieval Jewish commentators, clarified how they knew the time was not right at the first return:

> The return to Israel in the days of Ezra could have been like the first time the Jewish people entered Israel in the days of Joshua.... However, sin prevented this, for their repentance was imperfect. Since they were not worthy, they did not have permission to build the Temple, which was designated as the Temple for the eternal redemption, for when it will be built according to this design, the [divine] glory will rest upon it forever.

Only a small remnant of 50,000 Judeans (mixed also with remnants of Israelites) returned in 538 B.C. to rebuild the Temple. However, the work was delayed for 15 years because of foreign opposition. Also, Ezra and Nehemiah had to confront the sins of the people, which included spiritual apathy, unlawful marriages, violations of the Sabbath, and extortion. Further, we must remember that at that time the Jewish nation was not independent (as it had been during the First Temple) but was subject to the Persians. This subjugation continued throughout the entire time of the Second Temple under the Seleucids, Ptolemies, and finally the Romans, until these last rulers destroyed it in A.D. 70. In view of these historical realities, the glory (as described by Haggai) of the Second Temple was not greater than that of the First Temple.

Haggai's words in verse 9, "The latter glory of this house will be greater than the former," might at first appear to refer to a comparison between the First and Second Temples, but verses 6-7 make it clear that "this house" *cannot* be the Second Temple. According to these verses, the Temple described in verse 9 exists after a time of divine judgment in which earthly and heavenly disturbances force the Gentile nations to bring their wealth to the Temple (see Zechariah 14:14). Too, the "peace" in verse 9 is a universal peace. The prophet Isaiah (whose words were well-known to Haggai and the Israelites) tied this peace to the Temple and the end-time restoration:

> In the last days, the mountain of the house of the LORD will be established as the chief of the mountains, and will be raised above the hills; and all the nations will stream to it.... And He will judge between the nations, and will render decisions for many peoples; and they will hammer their swords into plowshares and their spears into pruning hooks. Nation will not lift up sword against nation, and never again will they learn war (Isaiah 2:2,4).

According to Tosefta *Yom Tov* (paragraph 60), the reason the future Temple would have a greater glory than the Second Temple was because the Second Temple had lacked five things that had been in the First Temple (one of these being the Ark), but these would be reinstated in the Third Temple. Even though Ezekiel 40–48 does not include the Ark in the descrirption of the final Temple, Binyan HaBayit (paragraph 34) explains that the prophet does not refer to the Ark here because the final Temple has dimensions and features different from previous Temples, and the Ark was the same Ark that had always existed in the Tabernacle and Temple.

In harmony with the biblical prophecies, most of the Jewish legends, as well as the traditions of the Samaritians, state that the Ark and the other original Temple vessels were hidden away in the providence of God to await the end times. The Jewish philosopher Philo, who lived in Alexandria, Egypt, during the first century, also attested that the sacred vessels were a treasure for all time. He explained that the Ark was made of non-decaying wood because it contained the incorruptible law and because it, along with all the furniture of the sanctuary and the Temple itself, "were ordained not for a limited time, *but for an infinite age*."[6] Whatever Philo's views about the last days, he believed that the Temple treasures were designed for all the ages.

The legends projecting the recovery of the Ark to the last days assured those in exile outside of Israel and those under Gentile domination within the Land that God's prophetic program had not gone wrong. It was still progressing on schedule. They were in effect saying, "What cannot be performed today will surely be accomplished tomorrow." However, we ought not to think that this was an apocalyptic panacea, a sort of psychological ploy to comfort those suffering hard times with an expectant but unrealistic hope. These writers fervently believed what the prophets of the past had predicted. They trusted that the God who had once given the order of worship—which required the Temple vessels—would not do less in the future and would restore all that had been lost. Their imaginative commentaries attempted to resolve unanswered dilemmas, such as what happened to the Ark. But neither these nor those in later rabbinic commentaries (the Midrash and Aggadah) lessen the Jews' literal understanding of the biblical prophecies concerning the rebuilding of the Temple. In our modern age we do not seem to consider a link with the past as necessary. We look for a brighter tomorrow built only off of today. This was not the case with our ancestors, and particularly not with those whose very heritage was rooted in the Promised Land. Professor P.R. Ackroyd explains:

> We are more prone in our contemporary situation to suppose that we can cut ourselves off from the past; the inhabitants of the ancient world were certainly not. And more than this, they were conscious of a need...that, whatever breaches with the past might occur, there should be a demonstrable link between the later and earlier stages of a community's life...if the life of the present and future was to be stable.[7]

So the assurance that God was watching over the Ark and other missing items gave a sense of connection with the eternal Israel, whose existence was unaffected by circumstance and whose return was guaranteed by an unconditional and everlasting covenant (see Genesis 17:7). This assurance also provided a sense of continuity with the glorious days of Israel's past, when the eternal and the temporal seemed to be one and the Temple and its worship were a holy witness to the world. When the regathering of Jews from around the world occurred, signaling the time of the redemption, Israel would rebuild the Temple and recover the hidden Ark and the Temple vessels. Then Israel could restore true worship and fulfill the prophetic promises of a restored nation (see Isaiah 2:2-4; 4:2-6; 11:6-16; 24–27; 60–66; Jeremiah 31:31-37; Ezekiel 36:18-38; 37:21-28) and particularly a restored Temple service (Jeremiah 33:14-18; Ezekiel 40–48; see Haggai 2:6-9; Zechariah 8:3-8; 14:16-21).[8]

Is There a Future for the Ark?

One passage seems to disagree with a return of the Ark in Israel's future: " 'It shall be in those days when you are multiplied and increased in the land,' declares the LORD, 'they will no longer say, "The ark of the covenant of the LORD." And it will not come to mind, nor will they remember it, nor will they miss it, nor will it be made again' " (Jeremiah 3:16). Old Testament scholar A.W. Streane commented on this verse, "The Ark, which had been the seat of the special manifestation of Jehovah, shall be forgotten, because the whole city shall be filled with His presence." Such an interpretation is typical of commentators who similarly conclude, "Jerusalem would be the throne of the Lord, a fact that would render the ark superfluous," or "This [is an] expression of antagonism to the Ark," or "The ark will not be restored because it will no longer be necessary as a symbol of God's presence."

Strangely, the author of the pseudepigraphal work the *Life of Jeremiah* (14-19) expected the Ark to stand at the center of the ingathered Jewish people in the end time after a period of persecution. He states that God will reveal the tablets of the law at this time of restoration, and that prior to this age a fiery cloud will hover over the Ark, "for the Glory of God will never cease from His Law." Why did this pseudepigraphal Jeremiah take this interpretation if he understood the original Jeremiah's prophecy to contradict it? However, the translation and interpretations given above do not necessarily stem from an understanding of the original text of Jeremiah 3:16-17. Translations of this passage differ in significant details and appear in many cases to have been influenced by the theological interpretations given it. A negative interpretation of the Ark in this context seems inconsistent with Jeremiah's other positive prophecies of Israel's restoration. The abandonment of the Ark, which testified to the law it contained, runs contrary to the strict standard of the law for Israel's conduct, which Jeremiah emphatically upheld (see Jeremiah 7:1–10:25). The Jewish commentator Abarbanel recognized this inconsistency and wondered how the Scripture could possibly have considered a promise that uprooted the Torah.

In order to understand Jeremiah's statements about the Ark in this future context, we need to look more carefully at his precise wording. First, Jeremiah repeatedly uses the phrase "they will no longer say" to indicate that an earlier phase of divine revelation will progress to a later one (see Jeremiah 23:7; 31:29). In each of these contexts, this progression clearly does not invalidate the previous revelation. Jeremiah is preparing the people for a period of transition without the Temple or Ark. He knew the inevitability of divine judgment and that God would remove both of these focal points of the divine presence. Therefore, he assured the people, who themselves would soon go into exile, that they, the Temple, and the Ark would one day be restored.

Jeremiah's statement concerning the Ark appears in a context that describes the promised future by comparing it to the past. Everything the past is not, the future will be. Disappointments will be reversed and fortunes restored. If the Ark was lost, the natural longing was for its return. What Jeremiah says is that not only will the Ark be restored, but also this restoration will be so great and extensive that no one will ever long for the Lord's presence again. The presence of the Lord, which was once limited to the Ark, will in that day fill the entire city of Jerusalem. The Ark is not excluded from this enlarged setting, as we see in the understanding brought to this text by Targum *Jonathan:* "Jerusalem shall be called the place of the house of the Lord's Shekinah." Instead of conceiving the whole city as God's earthly throne, Jerusalem will again house the Temple, which contains the divine presence. If this was the intended meaning of the original text, it would strengthen, rather than diminish, the possibility that the Ark would exist, since it would be properly included within that Temple.[9]

In order to further understand the nature of Jeremiah's statement, we can compare a similar statement in a restoration context in Isaiah 11:9: "They [wild beasts and reptiles] will not hurt or destroy in all My holy mountain [Jerusalem], for the earth will be full of the knowledge of the LORD as the waters cover the sea." So great will be the harmony in the created order because of the divine presence that normally predatory and poisonous creatures will become tame and harmless. This does not mean that these creatures will not exist or be present in the holy city, but that their function will be changed in the kingdom. We can say the same of the Ark. Because the glory of God fills the entire city (see Isaiah 4:5-6), no one will need to focus on the Ark as the sole place of manifestation. This, however, does not mean that the Ark will not exist or be present in the Temple, but that it will have a new function. It will no longer witness to the law, and it will no longer be a conduit of the divine power in warfare. The law will be internalized in that day (Jeremiah 31:33-34; Ezekiel 36:25-27), and the nations will no longer learn war (Isaiah 2:4). The textual notes of the Israeli military's standard issue Bible support this interpretation:

> The Law of the Lord will be written in the heart, and there will be no need to keep it in the Ark. There will not be wars and there will be no need to take the Ark from place to place on the battlefield as it was in those former times.

The perspective of the author of this commentary is that because Jerusalem in the future will come under a new covenant that transforms Israel and her enemies, the Ark will no longer need to function as in times past. One explanation for this is that Jeremiah 3:16 states, "...they will not *make* it again." This translation implies that the Ark was destroyed, and since neither the divinely inscribed tablets nor the graven cherubim could be remade, the Ark could not exist in the future. However, the translation "*make* it again" may not be a proper rendering of the Hebrew word *'asah* in this context. This verb generally does mean "to make" or "to do," but it also has other secondary meanings. One of these meanings is "to use," and significantly one of the two instances in which the verb appears with this nuance is in a context concerning the materials "used" in the construction of the Ark (Exodus 38:24; see 1 Samuel 8:16). Therefore, we can translate this last phrase in verse 16, "neither shall they *use* it again." In this case, the meaning is that Israel would not use the Ark as before in warfare because in the time of the restoration, war will be abolished (Isaiah 2:4). Israel would not use it as a witness to the law because in the future it will be written on their hearts (Jeremiah 31:33). We know the age to come is in view because the very next verse states that "at that time they shall call Jerusalem 'The Throne of the LORD,' and all the nations will be gathered to it, to Jerusalem, for the name of the LORD; nor will they walk anymore after the stubbornness of their evil heart" (Jeremiah 3:17). This plainly teaches that the change that will come to both Israel and the nations under the new covenant (Jeremiah 31:31-33) will remove the need for the Ark to function as it did under the Mosaic covenant. However, since the restored presence of God to Jerusalem will constitute it as "the throne of the Lord" the Ark will be associated with the divine glory as in the previous age (see Psalm 132:7-14; Ezekiel 43:1-7). Therefore, in harmony with a positive interpretation of the restoration prophecies, Jeremiah expects a future for Israel in which its worship will fulfill God's ideal—an ideal that may well include the restoration of the Ark.

Judaism's "Unforgotten" Ark

For all their long history since the destruction and dispersion of A.D. 70, the Jewish people have preserved the memory of the Ark. In every synagogue an "ark," in the form of a cabinet, takes center stage, holding all the Torah scrolls used in the service. Professor H.G. May makes this conclusion:

> We may ask whether the Jews really ceased to have any sacred ark of their own after the fall of Jerusalem.... It would be surprising if these arks did not preserve something of the form as well as of the function.... The ark in use in the early synagogues reflected a practice in the second temple which was, in turn, derived from the first temple.

Such Torah arks are always elaborately ornamented on the outside and hidden from public view by a decorated curtain bearing a rendition of the cherubim as two guardian lions. In some synagogues a lamp hangs before the Torah-ark called the *ner tamid* ("eternal light"), which symbolizes the Shekinah, the eternal presence of God. Since the Torah scrolls are the most expensive and important components of the synagogue, the Torah-ark remains the prized possession of the Jewish community. It is the one object throughout centuries of pogroms and holocausts that they have suffered and sacrificed to save. As such, it has borne a perpetual witness to the Jew of the forgotten but unforgettable Ark.

Even with this preservation in Judaism of the centrality of the Ark, the Torah-ark could not replace the Ark any more than the synagogue could replace the Temple. The synagogue has no priesthood and no sacrifices; it is simply a meeting place for a people who have lost their Temple and await its return. If, as the Jewish people expect—and the Scripture appears to promise—a new Temple will one day appear (Isaiah 2:2-3) in the day of Israel's redemption (Romans 11:25-29), why should not the Ark return as well to continue (in some measure) as a place for God's restored presence (Ezekiel 43:1-7)? Whatever we may decide concerning this future hope, we need presently to look beyond the symbol of the Ark to the substance of the promise it contains. This substance today constitutes the greatest search of modern man.

The Greatest Search

In this book we have been searching for the Ark of the Covenant. No conclusive evidence exists for the existence of the Ark, nor can its hiding place be definitively located. Yet our survey of the biblical, historical, and traditional sources provide sufficient warrant for us to conclude that the Ark still exists and could be discovered. Therefore, in answer to our question, Will the Ark ever be discovered? we can say that it is possible, but as the rabbi counseled, in the proper time.

The Ark may return some time in the future, but it points to a truth that is beyond time. The Ark was a mere container, designed to hold earthly witnesses to the eternal. As we have seen, because of this function as a witness of God's eternal covenant with Israel, God the eternal appeared at the Ark to confirm His word to His people. That word followed Israel into the depths of its sin against God, warning of the consequences of rebellion while promising the way to restoration. Despite all that Israel could do against God, the eternal covenant bound God through His word to remain faithful to Israel. After 70 years of captivity in a foreign land (because of their violation of the covenant), God would say to Israel, " 'I will visit you and fulfill My good word to you, to bring you back to this place. For I know the plans that I have for you,' declares the LORD, 'plans for welfare and not for calamity to give you a future and a hope' " (Jeremiah 29:10-11).

Surely God punished those people who sinned—and even the nation as it failed in its calling to be a light to the nations (Isaiah 49:6)—but still He sent that people and nation a Savior, One who would one day fulfill Israel's mission. The New Testament Gospel of John proclaims, "He [Jesus] came to His own [nation], and those who were His own did not receive Him. But as many as received Him, to them He gave the right to become children of God, even to those who believe in His name" (John 1:11-12). The Ark demonstrated God's desire to come to earth and to be with His people. Jesus came to fulfill this as Israel's Messiah and Deliverer from sin and the way to the promised restoration. In His day, thousands of Israelis believed in Him and received what He came to provide—the gift of eternal life with God. Many Gentiles also believed and, together with believing Jews, have come to form the church, the witness to God's word today. Perhaps for this reason it was appropriate that as the Second Temple period began—the era in which the Messiah was to appear (Daniel 9:25-26)—the Ark should disappear. However, just as the Messiah will return to complete His covenant with Israel, so the Ark may also return to remind the world in this future era of how well the Lord fulfills His word!

Perhaps the Ark of the Lord will eventually be recovered, but with lasting certainty the Lord of the Ark will soon appear. He is truly the lasting treasure at the end of every man's search, and you can experience His presence today. Since we have come this far together, may I ask you a personal question? Have you sought Him? Have you found Him? The same passage cited above concerning God's plans for Israel says, "Call upon Me and come and pray to Me, and I will listen to you. You will seek Me and find Me when you search for Me with all your heart" (Jeremiah 29:12-13). Jesus, the Glory of God, came into the world 2000 years ago to bear witness to the truth. He said, "I am the way, and the truth, and the life; no one comes to the Father but through Me" (John 14:6). If you will come to God, God says you must come through Jesus. As Savior, He died in the place of sinners in order to save them from the punishment of sin. As Redeemer, He paid the price to release sinners from the bondage of sin and into the freedom that belongs to the children of God. As the Risen Messiah, He lives to fulfill His promise to give eternal life to any who will take Him at His word. My prayer is that your search will end with the Savior, the greatest discovery of all!

Notes

Chapter 1—Understanding the Ark

1. Based on a standard cubit, the dimensions were 3'9" by 2' 3" by 2' 3". If the cubit was only five handbreadths (15"), the dimensions were 3' 1.5" by 1' 10.5" by 1' 10.5". According to Rabbi Getz, who made a measurement of the inner gates within the Warren's Gate, a cubit equals 57.8 centimeters. If this later cubit (used for the Second Temple) was the same as that used for the Ark, the measurements would be 3' 7" by 2' 2" by 2' 2".
2. It is a cognate with the Akkadian word *aranu,* which also means box or chest. The Hebrew word is used of the Temple money chest (2 Kings 12:9; 2 Chronicles 24:8-11).
3. The word means "box," or "container," but the context determines its specific connotation of "vessel."
4. See the description and references in Umberto Cassuto, *Commentary on Exodus* (Jerusalem: Magnes Press, 1967), p. 329.
5. See *Yoma* 72b; *Rashi; Ralbag.*
6. The Babylonian Talmud (*Yoma* 52b) adds the following items: a vial of anointing oil and the chest in which the Philistines sent a gift to the God of Israel (probably the golden models of the tumors and mice, which were connected with the Philistine plagues). However, the accounts of the Ark's contents in Deuteronomy 10:5 and especially 1 Kings 8:9 explicitly state that at this time only the tablets of the law were present.
7. The Old Testament, Josephus, and Philo are all unanimous in their verdict that the only items in the Ark were the tablets. The other two standard items—the jar of manna and Aaron's rod—were evidently kept in front of the Ark (Exodus 16:33-34; Numbers 17:10; 1 Kings 8:9; 2 Chronicles 5:10; see Philo, *De Vita Mosis* 2.97; Josephus, *Antiquities of the Jews* 3.6.5 #138; 8.4.1 #104.

8. Interview with Rabbi Shlomo Goren, Tel Aviv, January 25, 1994.
9. Flavius Josephus, *Antiquities of the Jews* 8.3.3.
10. "The Electrifying Ark," The Learning Channel (www.discovery.com/?channel=TLC).
11. Ibid.
12. Matthew Zymet, "Electric Artifact," The Learning Channel (www.discovery.com/?channel=TLC). Accessed October 13, 2004.
13. Henry Soltau, *The Holy Vessels and Furniture of the Tabernacle* (Grand Rapids: Kregel Publications, 1971), p. 28.
14. Michael ben Chaim, "Two Arks, Two Sets of Stones," *Mikdash-Build* 1, no. 3 (September 7, 1997).
15. See Rashi on Deuteronomy (called Devarim) 10:1-3 in *The Torah: With Rashi's Commentary Translated, Annotated, and Elucidated by Rabbi Yisrael Isser Zvi Herczeg,* The Artscroll Series (Brooklyn, NY: Mesorah Publications, Ltd., 2000), p. 98.
16. This tradition of the broken and complete tablets in the one Ark was so strong that rabbis used it as the basis of the moral principle that a scholar who has forgotten his learning is still entitled to respect.
17. The term *Shekinah*, the noun form of the root *skn* ("to dwell") first appears in the Jewish Targums. For example, Targum Onkelos paraphrases Exodus 25:8 this way: "Let them make Me a Sanctuary (Hebrew *mishkan*) that My Shekinah may dwell among them." Likewise, Targum Jonathan on 1 Kings 8:13 reads, "I have built the house of the Sanctuary for the house of the Shekinah forever." By rendering the personal statement of God dwelling with men by a word that emphasized the presence of God, the authors were apparently trying to avoid implying that God had a material body in these manifestations.
18. *The International Standard Bible Encyclopedia,* rev. ed., s.v. "Ark of the Covenant."
19. See *Interpreter's Dictionary of the Bible*, s.v. "Ark of the Covenant." G. Henton Davies notes that with the study of the symbolism of the Ark we are "in the presence of several parallel ancient ideas which largely overlap."
20. See H.G. May, "The Ark—A Miniature Temple," *The American Journal of Semitic Languages and Literatures* 52, no. 4 (July, 1936), p. 225.
21. See *Encyclopedia Judaica*, s.v. "Divination (in the Bible)."

22. The tenses of the verbs here are imperfects with *waw* consecutives and do not denote habitual or repeated action but rather something that occurred at a specific point in time.

Chapter 2—Fables and Facts About the Ark

1. Erich Von Däniken, *Chariots of the Gods* (New York: Bantam Books, 1971), p. 40.
2. Akiva Bernstein, "On the Parsha—the Spiritual Unified Field" *Mikdash-Build* 1-20, 7 Adar 5757 (1997).
3. Yelammedenu in Yalkut 1, 739; Wayekullu in Likkutim 2.17a-b.
4. Ibid. See also Sifre, Num. 85; Sifre, Zechariah 79; 193.
5. J.M.P. Otts, *Christ and the Cherubim; or, The Ark of the Covenant: A Type of Christ Our Saviour* (Richmond, VA: Presbyterian Committee of Publication, 1896), p. 21.
6. Henry Morris, *The Revelation Record: A Scientific and Devotional Commentary on the Prophetic Book of the End Times* (Wheaton, IL: Tyndale House 1983), p. 211.
7. From a letter to the editor by Spencer Brien in *Biblical Archaeology Review*, July-August, 1983, p. 31.
8. Revelation 15:5 combines all of the earthly sanctuaries into one as typifying the ideal heavenly model: "After these things I looked, and the temple of the tabernacle of testimony in heaven was opened." From the other uses of the heavenly Temple in Revelation we learn that the heavenly Temple houses an altar (6:9; 8:3,5; 9:13; 14:18; 16:7), God's throne (16:17), and the Ark (11:19). Some would also see the veil that separated the Holy Place from the Holy of Holies present in those texts which depict an "opening" to the heavenly throne room or Temple through which angelic beings or John himself passes immediately into the Divine presence (see Revelation 4:1-3; 6:14-17; 15:5; 16:1,17). See also J. Webb Mealy, *After the Thousand Years: Resurrection and Judgment in Revelation 20,* Journal for the Study of the New Testament Supplement Series 70 (Sheffield: JSOT Press, 1993), pp. 143-62,196-97.

Chapter 3—What Does Archaeology Reveal About the Ark?

1. Jordan Maxwell comment in the television documentary "Ancient Secrets of the Bible" (Desperado Films, Ltd., 1992).

2. See Alan Millard, "Tutankhamen, the Tabernacle and the Ark of the Covenant," *Bible and Spade* 7, no. 2 (Spring 1994), pp. 49-51.
3. See Elie Borowski, "Cherubim: God's Throne?" *Biblical Archaeology Review* 21, no. 4 (July-August 1995), pp. 36-41.
4. For a discussion of these evidences, see Roland de Vaux, "Les chérubins et l'arche d'alliance, les sphinx gardiens et les trônes divins dans l'Ancien Orient," *Mélanges de l'Université Saint-Joseph* 37 (1960-1961), pp. 91-124 and in English, his *Ancient Israel* 1, pp. 298-301.
5. See W.F. Albright, "What Were the Cherubim?" in *The Biblical Archaeologist Reader* 1 (Scholars Press, 1975), pp. 95-97.
6. The Old Testament, Josephus, and Philo are unanimous in their verdict that the only items in the Ark were the tablets. The other two standard items—the jar of manna and Aaron's rod—were kept in front of the Ark (1 Kings 8:9; 2 Chronicles 5:10; Numbers 17:10; Exodus 16:33-34; see Philo, *De Vita Mosis* 2.97; Josephus, *Antiquities* 3.6.5 #138; 8.4.1 # 104).
7. See Alan R. Millard, "Re-creating the Tablets of the Law," *Bible Review* 10, no. 1 (February 1994), pp. 49-53.
8. See the Babylonian Talmud *Baba Batra* 14a for this debate.
9. J.M.P. Otts, *Christ and the Cherubim; or, The Ark of the Covenant: A Type of Christ Our Saviour* (Richmond, VA: Presbyterian Committee of Publication, 1896), pp. 55-56.
10. Excerpt from recorded presentation given by Leen Ritmeyer at the annual meeting of the Near Eastern Archaeological Society, November 20, 1996, in Jacksonville, Mississippi.
11. Leen Ritmeyer, *The Temple and the Rock* (Harrogate, England: Ritmeyer Archaeological Design, 1996), pp. 24-25,41.
12. On Ritmeyer's views see also "The Ark of the Covenant, Where It Stood in Solomon's Temple," *Biblical Archaeology Review* (January-February 1996) and "Locating the Original Temple Mount," *Biblical Archaeology Review* (March-April 1992).

Chapter 4—Israel and the Ark

1. Rabbi Leibel Reznick, *The Holy Temple Revisited* (Lanham, MD: Jason Aronson, Inc., 1990), pp. 146-47.
2. The biblical text of 1 Samuel 6:19 gives the number slain as 50,070; however, this is generally conceded by conservative scholars as a copyist's error. The Greek translation of the Hebrew Old Testament reads 70, as does the

account given by Josephus, the first-century Jewish-Roman historian (*Antiquities of the Jews* 6.1.4).

3. See the discussion of this in Terence Fretheim, "The Cultic Use of the Ark of the Covenant in the Monarchial Period" (Ph.D. dissertation, Princeton Theological Seminary, 1967), p. 119.
4. I owe this insight to Eduard Nielsen, "Some Reflections on the History of the Ark," *Supplements to Vetus Testamentum* 7 (1959), p. 68, n. 2. However, Nielsen, following Galling, thought that the reason was that the Lord first dwelt between the cherubim at the Davidic inauguration and Solomonic installation. They believed that before this time the Lord was not attached to the Ark in any permanent manner.
5. Richard Elliot Friedman, *Who Wrote the Bible?* (London: Jonathan Cape Publishers, 1988), p. 156.
6. "The Disappearance of the Ark," *Israel Exploration Journal* 13 (1963), p. 46. Haran's book on *Temples and Temple Service in Ancient Israel* (Oxford, 1978) is a classic sourcebook in Temple study (although based on an assumption of the Documentary Hypothesis) and contains valuable material on the subject of the Ark.

Chapter 5—What Happened to the Ark?

1. See Benjamin Mazar, "The Campaign of Pharaoh Shishak to Palestine," *Supplements to Vetus Testamentum* 4 (1957), pp. 57-66.
2. Herbert G. May, "The Ark—A Miniature Temple," *The American Journal of Semitic Languages and Literatures* 52, no. 4 (July 1936), p. 220.
3. Menahem Haran, *Temples and Temple Services in Ancient Israel* (Oxford: Claredon Press, 1978), p. 285.

Chapter 6—Searches for the Ark

1. For the events of Parker's expedition see the fictionalized account by William le Queux, *The Treasure of Israel*, and a detailed report in *Jerusalem Underground: Discoveries on the Hill of Ophel, 1909–1911.*
2. These details were reported by Mrs. Bertha Spafford, widow of Hortio Spafford (who wrote the Christian hymn "It Is Well with My Soul"). Her observations of Parker's party are recorded in *Our Jerusalem* (1950), pp. 227-28.
3. Michael Sanders, "Arks of the Covenant, Part 3—Which Ark Is Found?" *Mysteries of the Bible*, 1997. (mike.sanders@biblemysteries.com)
4. Ibid.

Chapter 7—Is the Ark in Ethiopia?

1. Robert Cornuke and David Halbrook, *In Search of the Lost Ark of the Covenant* (Nashville: Broadman & Holman Publishers, 2002), p. 2.
2. For this see D.M. Master, "The Origin of Jewish Elements in Early Ethiopian Christianity," M.A. thesis (Miami University, Oxford, OH, 1995).
3. Edwin Yamauchi, *Africa and the Bible* (Grand Rapids: Baker Academic, 2004), p. 101.
4. Additional arguments against the Elephantine view may be found in Bezalel Porten, "From Jerusalem to Egypt: Did the Ark Stop at Elephantine?" *Mysteries of the Bible,* ed. Molly Dewshap Meinhardt, 2004, pp. 123-47.
5. As reported in the *Jerusalem Post International Edition* (October 3, 1992), p. 9. The purpose of Kaplan's book is to "demythologize" the history of Ethiopian tradition, since the 20 sacred apocryphal books of the Ethiopian community were only translated into Ge'ez (the community's liturgical language) from Arabic in the Middle Ages.
6. Harry R. Atkins, "Ark of the Covenant: Not in Ethiopia," Queries & Comments, *Biblical Archaeology Review* 19, no. 6 (November-December, 1993), p. 78.
7. Interview with Rabbi Shlomo Goren, Tel Aviv office, January 24, 1993.
8. Alfred Edersheim, *The Temple: Its Ministry and Services As They Were at the Time of Christ.* (Grand Rapids: Wm. B. Eerdmans Publishing Company, 1972), pp. 146-50.
9. Cornuke and Halbrook, *In Search of the Lost Ark of the Covenant,* p. 2.
10. Kaye Corbett, "Found: The Ark of the Covenant," *World Net Daily,* December 30, 1998.
11. As cited in Edward Ullendorff, *Ethiopia and the Bible* (Oxford: Oxford University Press, 1992), p. 83.
12. Roderick Grierson and Stuart Munro-Hay, *The Ark of the Covenant* (London: Phoenix, 2000), p. 257.
13. Interview with Fantahune Melaku, translated by Marv Asmare, Ethiopian Village, Jerusalem, January 27, 1994.
14. Grierson and Munro-Hay, *The Ark of the Covenant,* p. 341.
15. Ibid., p. 282.

Chapter 8—The Hidden Ark

1. Zohar Parshat, *Acharei Mot*, p. 67a; Parashat *Emor*, p. 102a.
2. The Jeremiah-Baruch traditions are complex, yet very similar. However, rather than one depending on the other, they both appear to go back to an earlier common source. See George W.E. Nickelsburg Jr. "Narrative Traditions in the Paralipomena of Jeremiah and 2 Baruch," *Catholic Biblical Quarterly* 35 (1973), p. 65.
3. For this argument see B.Z. Watcholder, "The Letter from Judah Maccabee to Aristobulus: Is 2 Maccabees 1:10b–2:18 Authentic?" *Hebrew Union College Annual* 49 (1978), pp. 89-133.
4. See also the Tannaitic idea of all things remaining "undecided" until Elijah comes (*'Eduyyot* 8:7; *Menahot* 45a).
5. For a thorough discussion of the Samaritan version see Marilyn F. Collins, "The Hidden Vessels in Samaritan Traditions," *Journal for the Study of Judaism* 3 (1972), pp. 97-116.
6. The Jewish Midrash on this text (Bereshit Rabbah 81:4 on Genesis 35:4) tells the story of a religious quarrel between a Jewish rabbi and a Samaritan. The rabbi brings up this verse and claims that the only reason the Samaritan worships on Mount Gerazim is because he is eager to get to the hidden idols beneath his site.
7. In the Dead Sea Scrolls (4Q Testimonia, 4Q 158 and 1QS IX, 11) a prophet like Moses also appears in a messianic function at the end of days.
8. For details see Cyril C. Dobson, *The Mystery of the Fate of the Ark of the Covenant* (Haverhill, MA: Anglo-Saxon Federation of America, 1939), pp. 59-96.

Chapter 9—Hidden Within History

1. Note that the word "then" in verse 19 connects the capture of the vessels to the fall of Jerusalem.
2. These were (1) the Ark, (2) the Holy Spirit (of prophecy), (3) the Urim and Thummim, (4) the holy fire, and (5) the Shekinah glory.
3. For details and references, see my book *In Search of Temple Treasures* (Eugene, OR: Harvest House Publishers, 1994), pp. 102-07,157-85,189-94.
4. Richard E. Friedman, "The Tabernacle in the Temple," *Biblical Achaeologist*, Fall 1980, p. 246.
5. *Yoma* 52b; Tosefta *Sotah* 13:2; Rav; Yer.

6. See Shekalim 6:1. Rabbi Hananiah was the last deputy high priest before the destruction of the Second Temple and lived sometime afterward. He is regarded by the Talmud as one who could give reliable testimony concerning the Temple practices (see Pesahim 14a; Zevahim 103b; Eduyyot 2:1-3).
7. See Shoshanim L'David; Yer; Tosefta *Sotah* 13:2; Rambam, Hil. Beit HaBechirah 4:1.
8. See Song of Songs Rabbah 3:3; Tifereth Yisrael; Radak (Kimchi) on 2 Chronicles 35:3.
9. See *Mikra U'Massores* and arguments based on *Chullin* 24a.
10. As recorded by the Roman historian Tacitus, *Historiae* 5.9.1.
11. Aryeh Kaplan, *Jerusalem: The Eye of the Universe* (New York: The National Conference of Synagogue Youth and the Union of Orthodox Jewish Congregations of America, 1984), p. 23.

Chapter 10—Is the Ark Under the Temple Mount?

1. Richard Andrews, *Blood on the Mountain: A History of the Temple Mount from the Ark to the Third Millennium* (London: Weidenfeld & Nicolson, 1999), p. 102.
2. Statement made at Sackville Faith Baptist Church as reported in "Delta Block: Ark of the Covenant Is in Jerusalem, and I Will Find It." www.paranormal.com/nuke/html/modules.php?name=news&file=articlessid=941. Accessed on November 23, 2004.
3. Interview with Rabbi Getz, January 25, 1994.
4. Interview with Dan Bahat (by Jimmy DeYoung), July 19, 1991.
5. This account is a composite account based on two separate interviews conducted with Rabbi Getz in his office June 23, 1993, and at the Warren's Gate, January 25, 1994.
6. Ibid.
7. Ibid.
8. Interview with Shlomo Goren (by Jimmy DeYoung), June 22, 1991.
9. Interview with Rabbi Chaim Richman, June 23, 1991.
10. Interview with Gerchon Salomon, Temple Mount Faithful office, January 23, 1994.
11. Interview with Shlomo Goren (by Jimmy DeYoung), June 22, 1991.
12. Interview with Dan Bahat at the Western Wall Tunnel, January 21, 1994.

13. Louis Rapoport, "The Mystery of the Real Lost Ark," *Jewish Digest* (September, 1982), p. 29.
14. Interview with Rabbi Getz, May 17, 1995.

Chapter 11—What Can I Believe?

1. My readers should be reminded that my critique of the published views of my fellow researchers and authors is not meant as a personal criticism but is part of the process of academic interaction through which all of our views can be refined.
2. F.J. Albers, "The Pyramid Tombs of Tanuatamun, Last Nubian Pharaoh and His Mother, Queen Qalhata," *KMT: A Modern Journal of Ancient Egypt* 14, no. 2 (Summer 2003), pp. 54-55.
3. Karol Mysliwiec, "The Saite Renaissance (Dynasty 26)," in *The Twilight of Ancient Egypt* (Ithaca, NY: Cornell University Press, n.d.), pp. 110-21; Nicolas Grimal, *A History of Ancient Egypt* (Oxford: Blackwell, 1992), p. 362.
4. Donald B. Redford, editor in chief, *The Oxford Encyclopedia of Ancient Egypt* 2, s.v. "Neco II."
5. Rosalie and Anthony E. David, *A Biographical Dictionary of Ancient Egypt*, s.v. "Neco II," "Psammetichus I," and "Psammetichus II" (London: Seaby, 1992).
6. Nicolas Grimal, *A History of Ancient Egypt*, p. 335.
7. For details on this see Abraham Malamat, "Josiah's Bid for Armageddon," *Journal of Ancient Near Eastern Studies* 5 (1973), pp. 274-78.
8. For further discussion on this issue see Sara Japhet, *I & II Chronicles, The Old Testament Library* (Louisville, KY: Westminster/John Knox Press, 1993), pp. 1041-44,1056-58. See also Rabbi Moshe Eisemann, *2 Chronicles, Artscroll Tanach Series* (New York: Mesorah Publications, 1992), pp. 317-19,460-61.
9. Edward Ullendorff, *Ethiopia and the Bible* (London: British Academy, 1968), p. 135.
10. Interview with Rabbi Shlomo Goren, Tel Aviv office, January 24, 1994.
11. Robert Cornuke and David Halbrook, *In Search of the Lost Ark of the Covenant* (Nashville: Broadman & Holman Publishers, 2002), p. 200.
12. Ibid, p. 203.
13. Michael A. Hiltzik, "Does Trail to Ark of the Covenant End Behind Axum Curtain?" *Los Angeles Times* (Tuesday, June 9, 1992), section H, p. 6.
14. Ibid.

15. "The Ark of the Covenant Discovered Near Jerusalem," *International Discovery Times* (June 2001), p. 4. This newspaper format publication was apparently the work of Jim Pinkoski, a commercial artist and associate of Ron Wyatt.
16. I have not talked directly with Wyatt, but I have spoken with pastors and laymen who had him present his findings in their church in 1992. This report is based on those conversations.
17. Video of Wyatt's excavation at Gordon's Calvary.
18. Jonathan Gray, *Ark of the Covenant* (South Australia: self-published, 4th printing 2000), p. 495.
19. Joe Kovacks, "Real-Life Raiders Hunt Ark of the Covenant," WorldNet Daily.com (August 16, 2003), p. 3.
20. This packet of materials is available from Dr. David Merling, Associate Director and Curator, Institute of Archaeology, Horn Archaeological Museum, Andrews University, Berrien Springs, MI 49104-0990 (hornmusm@andrews.edu).
21. Russell R. Standish and Colin D. Standish, *Holy Relics or Revelation* (Rapidan, VA: Hartland Publications, 1999), p. 11.
22. Ibid., p. 109.
23. This fact would, of course, disqualify this place as the site of Jesus' tomb, since the Bible notes that it was a "new tomb, in which never a man was laid," yet this tomb was used more than 600 years before the time of Christ.
24. For documentation on this matter please see chapter 16 "Archaeology and Jesus" in my book *The Stones Cry Out: How Archaeology Confirms the Truth of the Bible* (Eugene, OR: Harvest House Publishers, 1996), pp. 311-315.
25. On several different occasions before the writing of my 1994 book *In Search of Temple Treasures,* I requested a copy of the tape recording from Dr. Lewis. Although he insisted that it existed, he said it was lost among hundreds of such tapes that he made during his frequent trips to Israel. To my knowledge it has never been found, although its existence would still be useful in establishing the validity of the statement, since Hacohen himself denies he ever said it.
26. David Allen Lewis, *Prophecy 2000*, 6th rev. ed (Green Forest, AR: New Leaf Press, 1993), p. 176.
27. Interview with Rabbi Getz, office at the Western Wall, November 1996.
28. Interview with Rabbi Getz, office at the Western Wall, June 17, 1993.

Chapter 12—Will the Ark Ever Be Discovered?

1. *Sister Josephine and the Ark of the Covenant* (Jerusalem: Sisters of St. Joseph of the Apparition, n.d.), pp. 16-21.
2. Rabbi Leibel Reznick, *The Holy Temple Revisited* (Lanham, MD: Jason Aronson, Inc., 1990), p. 147.
3. Response to letter from Harold Jarrell, May 17, 2002.
4. *Voice of the Temple Mount* (November 1999).
5. Ibid.
6. *Questions and Answers on Exodus* 2.53 (which exists only in an Armenian version).
7. P.R. Ackroyd, "The Temple Vessels—A Continuity Theme," *Supplements to Vetus Testamentum* 23 (1972): 167.
8. For complete details on this subject see my book *The Desecration and Restoration of the Temple as an Eschatological Motif in the Old Testament, Jewish Apocalyptic Literature, and the New Testament* (Ann Arbor, MI: UMI Publications, 1994).
9. An objection to my interpretation was raised in a paper delivered at the Evangelical Theological Society in 1996 on the basis that the "throne of the Lord" was not the same as the "footstool of the Lord," the term used for the Ark of the Covenant (Psalm 132:7). But Ezekiel 43:7, a future restoration context involving the return of the Shekinah glory to the rebuilt Temple, uses the terms together of the same place, namely, the place of the Ark in the Holy of Holies where the presence of the Lord will appear and dwell among Israel forever. This is clearly the place of the Ark in the Holy of Holies, as we can see from a comparison with Ezekiel 9:3, which this passage completes (in restoration terms) by reversing the departure of the Shekinah from the condemned Temple. There the "glory of the God of Israel went up from the *cherub* [of the Ark] on which it had been." I agree that in Jeremiah 3:17 the term "throne" has in view the glorious rule of the Lord from a restored Jerusalem rather than focusing on a technical term for the Ark, although such need not exclude the Ark as part of this restored rule, as Ezekiel's text reveals.

Index

About the Author

Randall Price is regarded as one of the leading evangelical authorities on biblical prophecy and is recognized as an expert on the Middle East. He holds a master of theology degree from Dallas Theological Seminary in Old Testament and Semitic Languages, a Ph.D. from the University of Texas at Austin in Middle Eastern Studies, and has done graduate study at the Hebrew University of Jerusalem in the fields of Semitic Languages and Biblical Archaeology. He has taught undergraduate and graduate courses on biblical archaeology at the University of Texas, biblical languages at the Central Texas Bible Institute, and biblical theology at the International School of Theology.

As President of *World of the Bible Ministries, Inc.*, a nonprofit organization dedicated to reaching the world with a biblical analysis of the past, present, and future of the Middle East, Dr. Price speaks to international audiences through conferences and lectureships each year. He also serves as director of the Qumran Plateau excavation project in Israel, is a certified pilgrim tour guide in Israel, and through his tour company *World of the Bible Tours* has directed 45 tours to the Bible lands. Dr. Price has authored or co-authored some 20 books on the subjects of biblical archaeology and biblical prophecy, is general editor of *The Messianic Prophecy Bible* (in progress), and is a contributor to the *New Eerdmans Dictionary of the Bible.*

He has appeared on numerous television documentaries, including the "Ancient Secrets of the Bible" series, the "Thief in the Night" series, and "Uncovering the Truth about Jesus," has been the executive producer and on-screen host of five video productions based on his books. He is featured regularly on television and radio talk shows. Dr. Price and his wife, Beverlee, have five children and reside in Texas.

World of the Bible Ministries, Inc.

World of the Bible Ministries, Inc., is a nonprofit Christian organization dedicated to exploring and explaining the past, present, and prophetic world of the Bible through an analysis of archaeology, the Middle East conflict, and biblical prophecy. Three ministries comprise this organization to accomplish this practical purpose:

World of the Bible Productions—produces new books, online studies, and documentary films on biblical backgrounds and biblical prophecy for international outreach through distribution and media, and publishes the *World of the Bible News & Views* newsletter.

World of the Bible Seminars—the speaking ministry of Dr. Randall Price through conferences in churches and organizations, and college, university, and seminary lectureships.

World of the Bible Tours—Offers customized annual pilgrimages and study tours that allow participants to experience the reality of the world of the Bible.

To find out more about our products, request a free subscription to our newsletter, or receive a brochure of current tours to the Bible lands, or to contact Dr. Price for speaking engagements, you can reach us at:

Website: **www.worldofthebible.com**
E-mail: **wbmrandl@itouch.net**
Address: **World of the Bible Ministries, Inc.**
P.O. Box 827
San Marcos, TX 78667-827
Toll free (in US): **(866) 604-7322**
Phone: **(512) 396-3799**
Fax: **(512) 392-9080**

Other Books by Randall Price

The Battle For the Last Days' Temple

Many Jews long to rebuild the Temple destroyed in the Roman conquest of A.D. 70. But the site is now dominated by the Muslim Dome of the Rock and Palestinians claim the Jews have no previous history at the site. Randall Price provides fascinating answers based on archaeological evidence, historical records, and exclusive interviews with those at the forefront of the Temple movement.

The Coming Last Days' Temple

Rebuilding the temple? Surveying the plans, furnishings, priesthood, and research to replicate ancient Temple functions, Randy gives readers an up-close glimpse into preparations for prophecy fulfillment. Includes interviews with key officials. (Video and DVD also available.)

The Stones Cry Out

Recently uncovered ancient artifacts shed light upon the lives of the patriarchs, the Ark of the Covenant, the fall of Jerico, the existence of King David, and more. A fascinating survey of the lastest finds in Bible lands, with more than 80 photographs affirming the incontrovertible facts that support biblical truth. (Video and DVD also available.)

Secrets of the Dead Sea Scrolls

Discover the new technology that helps translators with previously unreadable Scroll fragments, supposedly "secret" Scrolls in hiding, the furious debate about who rightfully owns the Scrolls, and the newest efforts to find more Dead Sea Scrolls. Includes never-before-published photographs. (Video and DVD also available.)

Unholy War

Why does strife continue in the Middle East? How is it connected to terrorist attacks on Western nations? Dr. Price provides a concise, fascinating look at the problems and the players in the Middle East.

Fast Facts® on the Middle East Conflict

In a helpful Q-and-A format with maps, charts, and sidebars, bestselling author and expert in Middle Eastern studies Randall Price counters misconceptions with truth behind the headlines and a fascinating timeline of the conflict.

The Temple and Bible Prophecy

Are the biblical prophecies about a future temple merely symbolic, or do they point to a new physical Temple and even a restored sacrificial system? And are Israel's current, ongoing preparations to rebuild the Temple truly a significant sign of the end times? This comprehensive study of the Jewish Temple helps readers answer these questions and more.